YOU CAN MAKE DISCIPLES

YOU CAN MAKE DISCIPLES

GENE WARR

WORD BOOKS
PUBLISHER
4800 WEST WACO DRIVE
WACO, TEXAS
76703

To
IRMA

my loving companion and constant challenge to a greater depth of discipleship in my own life

ACKNOWLEDGMENTS

Some people seem to do quite well on their own, but I need all the help I can get. My deepest thanks to those who have made this book possible. First, to four of my dear friends, who insisted that the messages on discipleship be put into book form: Max Barnett, Billie Hanks, Ford Madison, and Wayne Watts. They never relented or let up. Secondly, to Monte Unger, who took the message transcriptions and put them into readable form. Thirdly, to those who read the manuscript and gave such helpful suggestions: Milton Bryan, and especially Keith Miller, who laboriously and painstakingly went over it line by line. Fourthly, to my secretary, Marty Townsend Olson, whose patience and perseverance through the many typings was a source of consistent encouragement to me. Then finally, to my editor, Al Bryant, whose spiritual sensitivity and technical excellence have added so much.

Contents

Foreword

Christians today are becoming more and more aware of the fact that they should be helping to fulfill Christ's Great Commission. They should be obedient to the command of Jesus to "go . . . make disciples."

Still, as in Jesus' day, the "laborers are few." Why? Some lack motivation. They simply don't seem to care very much. Others don't have a vision for what a layman should and can do. Many simply don't know how to go about it.

In this book, Gene Warr provides answers to the roadblocks that keep Christians from being effective. He motivates, provides vision, and shows step by step how to make disciples.

My friend Gene Warr is a disciplemaker. He is also a stimulator. He has been doing it for years and getting others to do it. Therefore, the material presented in this book has been tested in real life experience. It is a veritable handbook of how to's for those who are willing to obey Jesus' command to go and make disciples.

This book shows you that you *can* make disciples. I am happy to commend it and do trust it will have a wide circulation and use. Prayerfully applied to the lives and ministries of Christians today, these principles can help them become makers of disciples who will "turn the world upside down" (Acts 17:6).

—LORNE C. SANNY, President
The Navigators

1

Philosophy of Life

He was the shyest man I had ever met. Short and wide (this endeared him to me immediately), from the piny woods of east Texas, his looks and manners reflected his heritage. We would meet in the hallway of the church, and if I'd speak, he would blush, duck his head, and shuffle his feet. Although he was older than I, it seemed that God had given us an unusual and unique relationship. One day he asked if he might join my Sunday school class and if I would let him be the secretary so that he would not have to participate verbally. I agreed. Finally, he agreed to go visiting with me on the basis that I would do all the talking.

We spent month after month together calling on people I thought might be ready to become Christians. Between houses we'd share with each other and pray. One night, between visits, I asked Ted what he would do if someone would ask him to give his testimony. He ducked his head and replied, "I guess I'd just have to give it." It was only a few weeks later that I received an invitation to fill the pulpit in a church about a hundred miles away. I agreed to come if they would let me bring a four-man team. They agreed. I asked Ted to be one of the team members. The others of us who had been out before were really sweating him out, not knowing how or what he would do. We led off with an experienced man and then put Ted on.

Some months before I had given him a large, flexible leather-bound black Bible. He walked up to the pulpit and had to stand nearly on tiptoe to see over it. Doubling up that black Bible, brandishing it like a club, he said, "The reason most of us here are only 'nonimal' (he was trying for *nominal*) Christians is because we don't get into this book." I relaxed. His presentation was not flawless, his English was far from perfect, but the utter sincerity of his life carried his message straight to the hearts of the people in the congregation.

For years Ted had worked as a warehouseman for a large national department store chain. He made a comfortable living, had invested heavily in the company's savings, profit-sharing, and pension plans. A few short years later, Ted and his wife moved out of their comfortable home on the fashionable side of town and moved into an apartment over the mission center in the poorest section of our city. Why did they move? To minister to the disadvantaged and brokenhearted. A number of laymen joined hands and bought a used bus for Ted to use. Although he continued to work full time as a warehouseman, Ted found the time to drive the bus every Sunday and gather up the children in that ghetto area to bring them to the center. There he and his wife told them about Jesus. They all called him "Grandpa."

There is no way this side of eternity to know how many of those children and their parents found new life and hope through the ministry of Ted and his wife. What made the difference in Ted's life? The process we call discipleship.

In Ted we see the truth as expressed in Isaiah 60:22, "A little one shall become a thousand, and the small one a strong nation. . . ." Ted and his wife did not escape the tragedies and problems of life. Their only son died as a young man of a brain tumor, leaving behind his widow and two children. Their adopted daughter brought them deep heartache by rejecting their value systems in her own lifestyle. Still, they remained stedfast and faithful to the Lord.

The last year of their ministry before retirement was spent in an inner city church teaching those in need how to read, write, sew, care for children, keep house, and the many other things which most of us take for granted. Through it all, they taught others the love of God as expressed in Jesus Christ, and that each one as an individual is important and significant to God—and to Ted and his wife. Truly, in the words of Revelation 14:13, "Their works do follow them." Ted chose to take the road of discipleship which started with him embracing a meaningful philosophy of life and ministry.

Philosophy asks the age-old questions: What is man? Why is man? Where is he going? And I might add a more pragmatic question: What will he be *doing* while on the journey of life?

All over the world, people are looking for meaning and purpose in life. Boredom, frustration, and disappointment are everywhere. Many people want their lives to count for something, but don't know what to do to bring this about or even how to get started. One of the best places to start is with an overall philosophy of life. Once a life-goal has been established, the intermediate goals become more manageable. Thus, the first chapter in this book about being a disciple and a disciplemaker will be a brief outline of my personal philosophy of life.

R. Buckminster Fuller, philosopher, scientist and inventor of the geodesic dome, said, "Philosophy gains validity by the practical application of its general principles."[1] My philosophy is a *way of life*.

How one occupies one's time reveals what one is . . . and one's underlying philosophy of life. Everyone has a personal philosophy. Unfortunately, the word has been relegated to the dusty shelves of the library by some. Others think of philosophy as belonging only to the archaic words and thoughts of people like Plato and Socrates. And still others think of philosophy as being the incomprehensible utterances of the likes of Hegel or

Berkeley. Result: the word "philosophy" scares many.

It need not do so. It is a simple and true word which has come to mean in common terms, "a way of thinking about life which determines how one lives life." Each person, because we humans are thinking creatures, has a personal philosophy of life. It is in one's nature to have this. One may never have verbalized a philosophy; one may not know what philosophy is; but one moves through life, doing this and that. That personal philosophy, like an invisible steering mechanism at the very core of one's being, will guide a person and will manifest itself by action.

My personal philosophy for my spiritual ministry on earth can best be stated by what I once read in a religious newsletter: *"To know, love, and glorify God, and to be used of Him to raise up qualified laborers in significant numbers as fast as possible to help fulfill the Great Commission."*

To know God

In *The Pursuit of God* A. W. Tozer said, "It is inherent in personality to be able to know other personalities, but full knowledge of one personality by another cannot be achieved in one encounter. It is only after long and loving mental intercourse that the full possibilities of both can be explored."[2] It does take time to know anyone . . . and it takes a definite effort. Even a spouse of many years reveals new sides of his or her personality in the stresses of daily living.

Few of us know a President or a king personally. Think of what it would mean to be on intimate terms with such a person! Look at the many who wish to see, merely *see*, a famous movie star, a high-ranking political figure, an artist, or an athlete. And this says nothing of those who desire to be on intimate terms with such famous personages. People "name-drop" to impress others . . . and, perhaps, to boost their estimation of themselves in their own eyes.

Think of the inalienable privilege of "knowing God," the One who holds the universe together, the infinite and marvelous God. It is my great desire to know Him.

It was Paul's desire. He says:

> Yes, furthermore I count everything as loss compared to the possession of the priceless privilege—the overwhelming preciousness, the surpassing worth and supreme advantage—of knowing Christ Jesus my Lord, and of progressively becoming more deeply and intimately acquainted with Him, of perceiving and recognizing and understanding Him more fully and clearly. For His sake I have lost everything and consider it all to be mere rubbish (refuse, dregs), in order that I may win (gain) Christ, the Anointed One. . . . [For my determined purpose is] that I may know Him—that I may progressively become more deeply and intimately acquainted with Him, perceiving and recognizing and understanding [the wonders of His Person] more strongly and more clearly. And that I may in that same way come to know the power outflowing from His resurrection [which it exerts over believers]; and that I may so share His sufferings as to be continually transformed [in spirit into His likeness even] to His death. . . . (Phil. 3:8,10 Amplified).

The great people of the Bible and Christian history have had an insatiable hunger for God. But too few today really hunger for God. As Tozer says, "He waits to be wanted. Too bad that with many of us He waits so long, so very long, in vain."[3]

David, that great singer of Israel, the warrior-king, said, "The one thing I want from God, the thing I seek most of all, is the privilege of meditating in his Temple, *living in his presence every day of my life, delighting in his incomparable perfections and glory*" (Ps. 27:4 LB italics mine).

In Exodus 33:13, Moses said, "Now therefore, I pray thee, if I have found grace in thy sight, shew me now thy way, that I may know thee. . . ." Moses came to understand that really knowing God took place only in following the way of God. Therefore, he asked God to show him his way that he might know him.

To know God is imperative in the Christian philosophy of life. If we do not know Him, then we cannot love Him; and if we do not love Him, we will not trust Him; and if we do not trust Him, we cannot please Him. Hebrews 11:6 tells us, "But without faith it is impossible to please him. . . ."

It is also His desire that we know Him. When Adam and Eve sinned in the Garden and hid themselves from Him, it was God who took the initiative to find them. God asked, "Where are you, Adam?" God was seeking man. God says, "I don't want your sacrifices—I want your love; I don't want your offerings—I want you to know me" (Hosea 6:7 LB).

I was raised in a 50 percent Christian home. My mother took me to Sunday school and church, and my father worked and played hard. Both mother and dad were strong-willed people which led to some conflicts between them. Being the only child, I often found myself cast in the role of referee. I remember crying myself to sleep many nights as a young boy wondering if, when I woke up, my mother and father would still be together.

At twelve years of age, I walked the aisle and made what I assumed then was a personal commitment to Christ, which was the custom in our church. But I believe with all my heart that if I had died during the next ten years, I would have spent eternity separated from God. At the age of thirteen, by my own choice, I went away to military school. When you go to military school, one of two things has to happen: either you grow up, or you get out. So at the age of thirteen, I found myself playing the role of a grown-up. After graduating from military school, I was commissioned in the army at nineteen and found myself leading men in combat at the age of twenty. Prior to shipping overseas, I had married and we had a daughter.

During those days in Europe, my life could have been characterized as fearing neither God nor man. I was reckless with everything and every relationship in my life. On discharge from the army, I returned home to Oklahoma City. My father (who served in the Pacific in World War II) and I went into the building business together. This was in 1946 just after that war. Those who are old enough to remember will recognize the validity of this statement that after the War, people would do nearly anything except work. They might lie, cheat, and steal, but not work.

In the middle of July 1946, I went over to see what my competitor was building. There stood a huge man, driving nails with real fervor. The perspiration was pouring from him, and he was really doing a job. Forgetting my objective, I asked the building superintendent who the man was. He told me he was a carpenter. I explained to him that I could see that, but why did he work as he did? The superintendent told me he didn't know unless it was because he was a preacher. I then asked where he preached. He told me it was in a small 25 x 50 ft. building in the northwest part of our city, the mission of a large downtown church.

I decided that if the man could preach like he drove nails, then I'd go hear him. So the next Sunday morning found me on the way to the little building. When I drew near, I knew the services were going on because I could hear him singing. He had a large voice to fit his body. To this day, I believe that God rigged those sermons on me to get my attention (for which I will be eternally grateful). The man was not very well-educated, but two things he did know. One was the Bible and the other, the Lord Jesus Christ. And he preached both. While I do not remember all the details of the sermons, I do know the general outline.

The first Sunday, he preached on the fact of sin—that all have sinned and fallen short of God's measurement. That was a startling statement to me because I had always considered myself reasonably good, but thought perhaps I should clean up my life a bit.

The second Sunday, he preached on the penalty of sin, and that really was a frightening thought to me because if in fact all had sinned, then I stood in that position with everyone else. And the penalty did not look pleasant. He said it was eternal separation from God.

The third Sunday he told us that we could not do anything about our sins by trying to clean up our lives, by attending church, by embracing philosophy, or any of a number of things. And that didn't sound like good news to me; that sounded like bad news.

Finally, I believe it was the fourth Sunday, he explained that Jesus Christ had paid the penalty for our sins and that His substitutionary death on the cross could be effective in our experience if we would invite Him to come in and control our lives. For the first time in my life, I understood that the transaction which is called being saved or born again or redeemed or regenerated (all of which are good biblical terms) takes place not primarily in the intellect or the emotions, but in that part of our personality which God will not invade unless He's invited, namely the will.

That Sunday morning as an act of my will, I invited Christ to come in and control my life, and He did come in. Almost immediately I began teaching an adult Sunday school class and was spending from eight to ten hours a week preparing a thirty-minute lesson. But as I read and studied the Word of God, I recognized that there were vast areas of experience in the Christian life that I knew nothing about, and I didn't know why. Then in 1956 the Billy Graham Crusade came to Oklahoma City, and I was asked to be Co-chairman of Stadium Arrangements in charge of seating, lighting, the public address system, and so on.

I came to know the members of the Graham team well. There were two men on that team who took the time to put in my hands the tools necessary for a vital and dynamic walk with Jesus Christ every day. When I began approaching the Word of God, not from the standpoint of getting something for someone else, but simply to let Him speak to my own heart and condition, Jesus Christ became amazingly real to me. Instead of being Someone way off out there to whom one day I'll go, He became more real to me than most people around me, because I came to know Him better than I knew them. It was, in a sense, a transforming experience. I found that many of my most important objectives, goals, desires, and dreams were changing.

For the first time, I suppose, I realized that a Christian is a personal representative of God to those on earth who do not have a relationship with Him. We are, in fact, His ambassadors. In 2 Corinthians 5:20 Paul says, "Now then we are ambassadors for Christ. . . ." We must know Him to be able to represent Him. To be able to tell others about Him, we must know Him. We can't say much about a stranger. It is, therefore, imperative that we know God to be His disciple, and to be, in a real sense, a Christian . . . a Christ-one.

How do I get to know God?

I found that one of the key ways is through His words, which is one of the primary ways we get to know anyone. And in the pages of the Bible there is a total and complete revelation of God in Jesus Christ. Suppose we wanted to get to know a total stranger, but we had no evidence of anything he ever thought or said or did. We would have only a name, a name empty of words and facts and life. It would be an emptiness within a void, meaningless. We could make no move toward getting to know the stranger. But God has made it possible for us to get to know about Him: "Every Scripture is God-breathed—given by His inspiration—and profitable for instruction, for reproof and conviction of sin, for correction or error and discipline in obedience, and for training in righteousness [that is, in holy living, in conformity to God's will in thought, purpose and action], so that the man of God may be complete and proficient, well-fitted and thoroughly equipped for every good work" (2 Tim. 3:16,17, Amplified).

Study the Word. Become a master of the Word of God, for in it you will come to know Him. But there is no value in knowing the Word of God if we do not obey the Word of God. Let it master you as well. There is no substitute in the Christian life for obedience. Obedience is primarily a mind set.

My spiritual father in the faith heads up the counselor training and follow-up department of the Billy Graham team. His life of uncompromising obedience has been a constant challenge to me. For instance, in California, when he was out setting up one of the crusades and working in it, several mornings in a row the same waitress waited on him for breakfast. Her conversation became warmer and warmer as she told him of her divorce and the two children she had to raise, and how difficult it was. As soon as he recognized what was happening, he asked her the very next morning, "Do you know who I am?" She said no. He gave her his name and said, "I'm here to work in the Billy Graham Crusade and we're here to tell people about Jesus." This not only changed their relationship as a man and woman, but also allowed the opportunity to share with her the real answer to life's problems.

In another city, the hotel employed women elevator operators. His room was on the third floor. The operators dressed rather scantily and he thought that might possibly become a problem for him, so the rest of his stay, which was several months in duration, he never rode the elevator again. He simply walked up and down the three flights of stairs.

That is what is meant by a mind set for obedience. To know God in an intimate way, we must deal ruthlessly with temptation and sin.

There are some startling facts regarding obedience as pointed out in the Word of God. One, there is a time element in obedience. Delayed obedience is disobedience. In Psalm 119:59,60 David said, "I thought on my ways and turned my feet unto thy testimonies. I made haste, and delayed not to keep thy commandments."

Secondly, a vital walk with God requires obedience. In Amos 3:3, the writer asks, "Can two walk together except they be agreed?" If people aren't agreed, they're not going to do much walking together. That's rather like asking an ophthamologist to walk with an optometrist, or a medical doctor to walk with a naturopath, or a Russian to walk with a Chinese, or an Arab to walk with an Israeli. Obedience is necessary for meaningful fellowship with other believers. As 1 John 1:7 tells us, "If we walk in the light as he is in the light, we have fellowship one with another. . . ."

Thirdly, obedience is necessary for an effective prayer life. Isaiah 59:1 indicates that our disobedience causes God to turn His ear from us so that He will not hear. And David recognized in Psalm 66:18 that if he regarded iniquity in his heart, God would not hear him.

Fourthly, obedience is an important part of our whole duty as Christians. Ecclesiastes 12:13,14 tells us, "Let us hear the conclusion of the whole matter. Fear God and keep his commandments for this is the whole duty of man. For God shall bring every work into judgment with every secret thing whether it be good or whether it be evil."

In Deuteronomy 10:12,13 (LB), Moses asks, "And now, Israel, what does the Lord your God require of you except to listen carefully to all he says to you, and to obey for your own good the commandments I am giving you today, and to love him, and to worship him with all your hearts and souls." Micah says, "He hath shewed thee, O man, what is good; and what doth the Lord require of thee, but to do justly, and to love mercy, and to walk humbly with thy God?" (Micah 6:8).

Fifthly, obedience is the proof of our love. In John 14:21, Jesus said, "He that hath my commandments and keepeth them, he it is that loveth me. And he that loveth me shall be loved of my Father, and I will love him, and will manifest myself to him." When we choose to disobey God, we are saying one of two things to Him: either, "God, You do not have my best interest at heart." (When we do this, we ignore Jeremiah 29:11, where He said, "I know the thoughts that I think toward you . . . thoughts of peace, and not of evil, to give you an expected end.") Or we're saying to Him, "God, You do not know what is best for me." To say that, we must ignore Paul's statement: "And he has showered down upon us the richness of his grace—for how well he understands us and knows what is best for us at all times" (Eph. 1:8 LB).

A fair question might be, "What are the results of knowing God?" To know Him is to become like Him and to please Him. The Bible says, "Enoch was sixty-five years old when his son Methuselah was born. Afterwards he lived another 300 years in fellowship with God and produced sons and daughters; then when he was 365, and in constant touch with God, he disappeared, for God took him!" (Gen. 5:21–24 LB). Yet in Hebrews 11:5, we read these words, "By faith Enoch was translated that he should not see death; and was not found, because God had translated him; before his translation he had this testimony, that he pleased God." We don't know all that Enoch did. As far as we know, he never preached a sermon, never attended church, or never memorized a scripture, but we do know he walked with God. Someone, using his imagination, has said that Enoch and God were so used to walking together in the evenings that one night God simply said, "Enoch, I believe we're closer to my house than we are yours. Why don't you just come on home with me?" And he did. We know that Enoch's intimate relationship with Him was pleasing to God.

Yes, we get to know Him through His Word; we get to know Him by spending time with Him; but we also get to know Him through the example of godly people. A story is told of something that happened one winter in a large city in Illinois. A little street urchin was standing with his face pressed against the show windows of a large department store looking longingly inside. He had on a thin pair of pants, a threadbare shirt, no cap, no jacket, and his feet were wrapped in rags which were stained with blood, undoubtedly from his frozen and cracked feet. Unlike most little boys, he was not looking at the toys in the window, but he was looking at a pair of insulated boots.

About that time, a limousine came down the street. It stopped in front of the department store and the chauffeur helped a very elegantly dressed lady out of the car. She saw the boy at the window and immediately knew what the situation was. Approaching the lad she said, "Son, why don't you come in with me?" Taking him inside the store, she began to outfit him. She bought him some thermal underwear, some wool socks, some warm trousers, a plaid wool shirt, one of those caps with ear flaps you can pull down over your ears, and a pair of warm fur-lined gloves. Finally, she bought him that pair of insulated boots.

When he was dressed and was just lacing up the last boot, he looked up at her and asked, "Lady, are you God's wife?" She said, "No, son, but I'm one of His daughters." We come to know God many times through the example of His people. But the basic way we get to know Him is through spending time with Him in His Word.

Should we as Christians be any less armed with the words of our Master than the Chinese communists are armed with the words of their self-proclaimed master? Millions of copies of a little red book entitled *Quotations from Chairman Mao Tse-tung* have been printed. In the foreword, the editors have written, "In studying the works of Chairman Mao, one should have specific problems in mind, study and apply his works in a creative way, combine study with application, first study what must be urgently applied so as to get quick results, and strive hard to apply what one is studying. In order really to master Mao Tse-tung's thought, it is essential to study many of Chairman Mao's basic concepts over and over again, and it is best to memorize important statements and study and apply them repeatedly. . . . study Chairman Mao's writings, follow his teachings, act according to his instructions and be his good fighters."[4]

Can we do any less as Christians? I want to know God and am attempting to get to know Him better every day by studying His words, by spending time with Him, and by following the examples of others who knew Him. We become like the people with whom we spend time. The wise writer of Proverbs says, "He who walks with wise men becomes wise . . ." (Prov. 13:20 RSV).

To love God

It is one thing to know a person; it is another to love him. One may discover in getting to know another that he can't love him. However, knowing God *only* leads to loving Him.

Strangely, the first reason we should love God is that we are commanded to do so. On the human scale we can't "command" another person to love us, though it would certainly simplify some relationships. How can God command us to love Him?

He does so in Matthew 22:36–40, where the writer records the following conversation: "Master, which is the great commandment in the law? Jesus said unto him, Thou shalt love the Lord thy God with all thy heart, and with all thy soul, and with all thy mind. This is the first and great commandment. And the second is like unto it, Thou shalt love thy neighbour as thyself. On these two commandments hang all the law and the prophets."

God will never give us a command which we are incapable of obeying or that is bad for us. We must believe this. God did not give us the option to love Him or not; He commanded it. In the midst of the complexities of earthly life, He knew that we would need to love Him. He made a great effort to give us this commandment; in fact, out of all the commands and laws and rules in the Scriptures, He labels this one as the first and most important. It is the sum of all the commandments.

An important clue as to why we should obey this commandment and love God is given in Deuteronomy: "Look, today I have set before you life and death, depending on whether you obey or disobey. I have commanded you today to love the Lord your God . . ." (Deut. 30:15,16 LB). Then in the twentieth verse of the same chapter, the Bible says, "Choose to love the Lord your God and to obey him and to cling to him, for he is your life. . . ." There is *life* in obeying the commandment to love God.

Knowing our fragility and continuing bent toward sinful straying, He knows that if we do not choose to love Him we will have miserable lives. "Turning to other idols" has been the downfall of many, but to love God is to choose life. Jesus speaks of this life in John 10:10 with the fulfilling adverb, "abundantly." He said, ". . . I am come that they might have life, and that they might have it more abundantly."

So God can command us to love Him, because He always has our best interests at heart. Paul says, ". . . and he has showered down upon us the richness of his grace—for how well he understands us and knows what is best for us at all times" (Eph. 1:8 LB). And Jeremiah records: "For I know the plans I have for you, says the Lord. They are plans for good and not for evil, to give you a future and a hope" (Jer. 29:11 LB).

Thus, when the Lord said in the first of the Ten Commandments, "You may worship no other god than me," and "I will not share your affection with any other god" (Exod. 20:3,5 LB), He meant it. Other gods and idols kill our affection for Him. They dilute our love for Him. Our source of love-strength is debilitated, for it is spent in too many directions.

I want to love God more day by day and to experience in a deeper way the abundant life Jesus promised. Don't you?

However, loving God is not always an easy matter. In 2 Kings 17:33, we read, "They feared the Lord, and served their own gods." The result was that the king of Assyria, who was populating the cities of Samaria, found that the lions were multiplying and eating up the people. Yet some people today hang onto some of their old idols which really quench their love for God and reveal their lack of love for Him. We can all recognize some of the idols: pride ("*I* can do it") in ability, family, heritage, intelligence, possessions, looks, strength. We forget that 1 Corinthians 4:7 says, "Who maketh thee to differ from another? and what hast thou that thou didst not receive? now if thou didst receive it, why dost thou glory, as if thou hadst not received it?" The teaching is: whatever we have—whether it's a good personality, a strong body, or a good mind—is a gift to us by God. It is not something we manufactured ourselves.

Secondly, there is the idol of bitterness. In Hebrews 12:15 the writer says, "Looking diligently lest any man fail of the grace of God; lest any root of bitterness springing up trouble you, and thereby many be defiled." I know a dear lady who has been raised in the church. She has tremendous abilities and talents, is well equipped with the Word of God, has been used of God in helping many in years past—but today she finds herself on the shelf outside the will of God. The only discernible reason that I can see is a root of bitterness which sprang up some years ago and has totally paralyzed her as far as effectiveness in the kingdom is concerned. Not only has it affected her, but it has also affected her family and all those with whom she comes in contact. Truly, bitterness is that idol which defiles many.

A third idol is the one of prosperity and success. We don't believe what Jesus said in Luke 12:15, "A man's life consisteth not in the abundance of the things which he possesseth." Unfortunately, many men's love for God grows or decreases in the opposite proportion of their Dunn and Bradstreet rating. As their Dunn and Bradstreet rating goes up, their love for God goes down. As the Dunn and Bradstreet rating goes down, their love for God goes up. In a spiritual sense, it's often more difficult to survive prosperity than it is poverty.

We're very familiar with the fourth idol—that of self-seeking. Yet in Jeremiah 45:5 the Bible says, "Seekest thou great things for thyself? Seek them not." Our love for God should not emerge out of a fear of the consequences, or simply from what he can do for us. They tell the story of an old woman who was seen coming along the streets of Strasboerg a great number of years ago. She was carrying a pail of water in one hand and a torch in the other. When asked what she was about, she answered that with the pail of water she was going to put out the flames of hell, and with the torch she was going to burn up heaven, so that in the future, men could love the dear Lord God for Himself alone and not out of a fear of hell or out of a craving for reward. We show our love for God by obeying Him, by desiring His presence, and by loving others.

To glorify God

What does it mean to "glorify" God, *why* should we glorify Him, and finally, *how* can we glorify Him?

"Glorify" is a word seldom used in everyday language today. Men sometimes use it in praising their business or organization, saying it is the greatest and the most wonderful . . . and they are generally put down with "Don't glorify it so; it isn't all that great." So the use of the word in common context is not encouraged. The word is far too magnificent in connotation for common usage.

The Random House Dictionary of the English Lan-

guage says "glorify" means " . . . to magnify with praise, to extol, to transform into or treat as more splendid, more excellent than would normally be considered."

Therefore, to glorify God is, in action and words, to pointedly refer to Him in an extremely magnifying manner. Helen of Troy had such beauty that "her face launched a thousand ships." She was so lovely and so desirable that her beauty alone compelled tens of thousands of men to move into action because of her. They were "glorifying" her—treating her as more splendid than was normal in the treatment of even the most beautiful of women.

And so . . . God wants us to refer to Him in glorifying magnificence.

Why? First, it is *the purpose for which we were created.* Isaiah 43:7 tells us, "Even every one that is called by my name: for I have created him for my glory, I have formed him; yea, I have made him." And John says, "Thou art worthy, O Lord, to receive glory and honour and power; for thou has created all things, and for thy pleasure they are and were created" (Rev. 4:11).

Second, *we are commanded* to glorify God. "Whether therefore ye eat, or drink, or whatsoever ye do, do all to the glory of God" (1 Cor. 10:31). We have already seen that we can trust God's commands.

Third, by getting to know and love God, *one can not help but glorify Him.* This will come as a natural consequence, for He is great and worthy of far more praise than we can give Him.

God created the universe and all in it, from the smallest to the greatest. A hydrogen atom is one-billionth of an inch in diameter. The metagalaxy is more than 1,000 million trillion miles in diameter.

According to Harlow Shapley, former Director of the Harvard College observatory, to count the atoms in a single breath would require 1,000 men counting 100 atoms a second, 8 hours a day, for about 10 billion years.

That is an example of God's creativity in the micro-world. In the other direction, Shapley estimates that there are *at least* 100 thousand million billion stars in our universe.

There *is* reason to glorify God. We cannot help but glorify Him with each breath we take and with each new glimpse of the heavens.

But how can we glorify God? First of all, *by praising Him.* Psalm 50:23 says, "Whoso offereth praise glorifieth me: and to him that ordereth his conversation aright will I shew the salvation of God." I do not understand how the lips of mortal man can offer praise to an infinite and holy God and thereby glorify Him, but that's what the Bible says.

Secondly, we can glorify God *by our conscious actions.* In 1 Corinthians 10:31 we're admonished, "Whether therefore ye eat, or drink, or whatsoever ye do, do all to the glory of God." But also, we can glorify God unconsciously: "When Jesus heard *that* (Lazarus's sickness) he said, This sickness is not unto death, but for the glory of God that the Son of God might be glorified thereby" (John 11:4). Lazarus was glorifying God unconsciously.

Thirdly, we can glorify God *by bearing fruit.* In John 15:8 Jesus said, "Herein is my Father glorified, that ye bear much fruit; so shall ye be my disciples." The two kinds of fruit spoken of here are first of all, the fruit of the Spirit in our own lives. Galatians 5:22,23 lists them: "But the fruit of the Spirit is love, joy, peace, longsuffering, gentleness, goodness, faith, meekness, temperance. Against such there is no law." And then also the fruit of other people coming to know Christ in reality. In John 15:16, the Master said, "Ye have not chosen me, but I have chosen you, and ordained you, that ye should go and bring forth fruit."

Fourthly, we glorify God *by believing Him:* "No distrust made him waver concerning the promise of God, but he grew strong in his faith as he gave glory to God" (Rom. 4:20 RSV). When we believe God, we glorify Him.

Fifthly, we glorify God *by declaring Christ Jesus as Lord of our lives.* Philippians 2:11 tells us, "And that every tongue should confess that Jesus Christ is Lord, to the glory of God the Father." And whenever a tongue confesses that Jesus is Lord, the Father, God, is thereby glorified.

Sixthly, we glorify God *by what we are.* In Ephesians 1:12 Paul says, "That we should *be* to the praise of His glory, who first trusted in Christ."

To be used by Him.

After one gets to know Him, love Him, and is led irresistibly to glorify Him, think of the marvelous privilege of "being used by Him." This isn't referring to our work. It is not a job or a profession . . . it is an honor. And every Christian can be used by Him.

Don't be misled. We don't produce the results in the Christian ministry, for the Bible indicates that God does the work. Only He produces spiritual results: "Except the Lord build the house, they labour in vain that build it . . ." (Ps. 127:1). "I am the vine, ye are the branches: He that abideth in me, and I in him, the same bringeth forth much fruit: *for without me you can do nothing*" (John 15:5, italics mine). Jesus said in John 6:63, "It is the spirit that quickeneth; the flesh profiteth nothing. . . ." In 1 Corinthians 3:6 Paul said, "I have planted, Apollos watered; but God gave the increase." In 2 Corinthians 10 in *Letters to Street Christians* we read, "We don't have to be concerned about how great we look in men's eyes. The Father has a plan for each one of us in building up His family. He gives us the work to do, and He's the one that does it."

God does need to use instruments on earth to do His work, and He has chosen to work through us. But He can only work through us if we're *available* to Him. We must be willing to be used. Haggai 2:19 asks, "Is the seed yet in the barn?" That's too true in many of our lives. God has invested much in us, but we seem either unable or unwilling to share with others. Then we must be *fit* to be used. In 2 Timothy 2:19–21 Paul indicates that there are many vessels in a house—some to honor and some to dishonor—that we should purge ourselves of the sins in our lives in order to be a vessel fit for the Master to use. Further, we must be equipped. Paul says, "The scriptures are the comprehensive equipment of the man of God, and fit him fully for all branches of his work" (2 Tim. 3:17 Phillips).

Note that the first three parts of the philosophy (knowing, loving, and glorifying God) have to do with character. What we *are* is more important than what we *do*, for what we *are* will determine what we will *do*. God is more interested in *making* us into something, than He is in simply *teaching* us something. Our character must be right in order for us to fulfill His purpose for us.

To raise up qualified laborers

Jesus commanded that we pray for this: "But when he saw the multitudes, he was moved with compassion on them, because they fainted, and were scattered abroad, as sheep having no shepherd. Then saith he unto his disciples, The harvest truly is plenteous, but the labourers are few; pray ye therefore the Lord of the harvest, that he will send forth labourers into his harvest" (Matt. 9:36–38).

A qualified laborer is a person who:

1. Knows what the objective is. Activity is no substitute for productivity. Oliver Cromwell said, "No one has gone so far as the man who doesn't know where he's going."

2. Is equipped to do the job. In the days when I was working as a trim carpenter we carried our tools in a large wooden box with a half-inch gas pipe as a handle. It was a real challenge just to haul the tools around. One day the superintendent hired a man, and he came to work with his set of tools in a box only a little larger than a square lunch box. We really had fun laughing at him coming to work with such a little box of tools.

He took it good naturedly, replying in his broken English, as we continued the fun, until it came time to go to work. Then he opened his little box of tools and began to put up casing. He had a little saw that looked like a small meat saw. Cutting the joints, he put the sides and the heads together. Whenever he did, the joint looked like it had grown there. Since he was accomplishing twice as much as any of the rest of us, we stopped laughing. We came to understand that the man was equipped to do the job and had the tools he needed. And so it is with qualified laborers. A qualified laborer is skilled and equipped to do the job.

3. He is also committed to getting the task done. When the other soldiers laughed at an Athenian soldier who was crippled, he silenced them by saying, "I came here to fight, not to run."

Where are these laborers going to come from? They are going to be raised up through you and me. The Bible is explicit on this: "And they that shall be of thee shall build the old waste places: thou shalt raise up the foundations of many generations; and thou shalt be called, The repairer of the breach, The restorer of paths to dwell in" (Isa. 58:12).

This is the action center of my life philosophy: to raise up qualified laborers. To me "to raise up" means to recruit, teach, train, and build. "Laborers" means disciples. This is disciplemaking, the subject of my book. To reach the lost of the world we must make disciples who will be equipped to go out and spread the good news of Jesus Christ.

In 2 Timothy 2:2 Paul points out four generations of disciples: "And the things that thou hast heard of me among many witnesses, the same commit thou to faithful men, who shall be able to teach others also." The four generations are "Paul"; "Timothy," the man Paul personally taught; "faithful men," those whom Timothy reached and trained; and "others," men reached by the faithful ones Timothy raised up. Who are you reaching? Who are you raising up?

These laborers are raised up one by one. Recently I was

reading the list of David's thirty mighty men in 2 Samuel 23. Verse 37 stood out to me in a way I'd never seen before. It said, "Zelek the Ammonite, Nahari the Beerothite, armor-bearer to Joab the son of Zeruiah." I wondered what in the world an armor-bearer was doing among David's thirty mighty men. Joab was the general of the army and probably had his choice of all the armorbearers. Since an armor-bearer in those days was like a wing man in a flight of airplanes in a squadron today, I expect he chose his man very carefully. But I can also see Nahari watching Joab's every move—the way he handled himself defensively with his shield, his footwork, the way he used his sword and spear, and perhaps at night Nahari would be out in the barn practicing with Joab's weapons. He would thrust and parry and really work at copying what he saw this master fighter do.

Then it may have been that one day while the battle was going on and waxing hot David saw Joab and Nahari in the battle, and said to the man with him, "Who is that next to Joab?" The man replied, "Why, that's Nahari, the Beerothite, Joab's armor-bearer." David said, "Why, he fights just like Joab used to when he was younger. Let's take him to be one of our thirty mighty men." How did Nahari become that proficient? By spending time with Joab. Watching him, working with him, copying him, imitating him until he became a mighty warrior. There are two questions which you should answer for yourself at this point in the book. One—whose armor am I carrying? And two—who is carrying my armor?

A key motivation in my life is to give myself to the making of disciples who will continue a chain of spiritual multiplication by reproducing themselves in others.

In significant numbers

There can be considerable danger in emphasizing "numbers." Some churches and organizations play the numbers game: the number of baptisms, attendance figures, the size of the budget, new programs. Those are all merely measuring sticks.

But there is a sense in which numbers are important, for they represent people. Numbers represent souls . . . and every individual on earth has worth and is significant. There are no insignificant persons in the kingdom of God. We do need a large number of qualified laborers because of the vastness of the harvest. "The harvest truly is plenteous, but the labourers are few" (Matt. 9:37). There is a labor shortage, not a harvest shortage. And part of my personal philosophy is to help reduce the labor shortage.

As fast as possible

Why should this emphasis on speed be in one's philosophy of life? A friend of mine who saw it disliked this part of my life objective. But the reason it is here is twofold: one is the tremendous need and the other is the shortness of time.

In Ephesians 5:15–17 Paul says, "Live life, then, with a due sense of responsibility, not as men who do not know the meaning and purpose of life but as those who do. Make the best use of your time, despite all the difficulties of these days. Don't be vague but firmly grasp what you know to be the will of the Lord" (Phillips).

There is a poem entitled "Redeeming the Time":

> I have only just a minute,
> Just sixty seconds in it,
> Forced upon me, can't refuse it,
> Didn't seek it, didn't choose it.
> I must suffer if I loose it.
> Give account if I abuse it,
> Just a tiny little minute,
> But eternity is in it.
> *Unknown*[5]

One can lose money, but he can make more of that. There are no reissues on time. An Arabian proverb says,

"Four things come not back: the sped arrow, the spoken word, time past, and opportunity lost."

It takes time, much time, for Christian disciples to mature. There are no instant disciples. No instant answers. No instant maturity.

When God builds a mushroom He does it overnight, and it dies overnight. But when He wants to build an oak tree, He takes time. God is not building His children into mushrooms; He is building them into oaks, so they can stand against the temptations and the wiles of Satan and against the winds of circumstance that blow and beat upon them.

We have the incomparable privilege of helping people become available to God so that He can grow them into the mature disciples He wishes them to be.

Here are the names of some familiar believers whom God obviously brought to maturity and used for His glory: A. T. Pierson, J. Wilbur Chapman, F. B. Meyer, Andrew Murray, Francis Ridley Havergal, Adolph Saphir, Amy Carmichael, and E. Hopkins. These men and women invested an average of fifteen years of their lives in Christian work before they began to know Christ as Lord. At that point they ceased to try to work for Him and began allowing Him to be their all and all—to do His work through them. We can't find maturity in thirty minutes, or one year, or eighteen months. It just doesn't happen that way. It takes time. As I sit here working on this manuscript today, if I live my three score and ten, that is, 70 years, I have 6394 days left. That means that 75 percent of my life is behind me. A little less than 25 percent is ahead of me. Three out of every four days of my life have already been lived. Therefore, if I'm going to do anything, I really need to get started. Time is too short for me to be putting in the strokes where they do not count. How about you?

To help fulfill the Great Commission

Here it is: the great direction toward which every Christian ought to be aiming his life. There are numerous biblical references which proclaim the Great Commission (Matt. 28:19,20, Mark 16:14,15, Luke 24:44–49, John 20:19–33, and Acts 1:8). In Matthew Jesus says, "Go therefore and make disciples of all nations, baptizing them in the name of the Father and of the Son and of the Holy Spirit, teaching them to observe all that I have commanded you; and lo, I am with you always, to the close of the age" (RSV).

There are two parts to the Great Commission: one is winning men to Christ, and the other is making disciples.

I would like to call to your attention a significant and often overlooked verse: "And when he (Jesus) was come near, he beheld the city, and wept over it" (Luke 19:41). Jesus wept. He was sitting on a hilltop in Jerusalem. Looking out over the houses sprawling on the hillsides and seeing the people milling in the streets and lanes, He was so moved with compassion that He cried. This is the spirit of the Great Commission. There is a world of cities out there, with people wandering about and searching for answers and living in despair . . . nearly four billion of them. The Great Commission compels me, and you, and all Christians to go and make disciples, to go and tell the good news of abundant life in Christ . . . to *go* and *do*.

But if we're to do this by making disciples, then what does one look like? Where's the blueprint? In the next chapter, we will see the specifics.

NOTES

[1]Alden Hatch, *Buckminster Fuller: At Home in the Universe,* (New York: Crown Publishers Inc., 1974) p. 184.

[2]A. W. Tozer, *The Pursuit of God* (Harrisburg, Pa.: Christian Publications Inc. 1948) p. 13.

[3]*Ibid,* p. 17.

[4]Quotations from Chairman Mao Tse-tung (Peking: Foreign Languages Press, 1968), from the Foreword, p. ii.

[5]Quoted from *The Encyclopedia of Religious Quotations* (Old Tappan, N.J. : Fleming H. Revell, 1976).

2

Qualifications for Discipleship

If God, through Christ, has commanded us to raise up disciples, as He did so command in the Great Commission, then it is imperative for us to know who a disciple is.

The *Random House Dictionary of the English Language* defines a disciple as "one who is a pupil or an adherent of the doctrines of another." Therefore, *a disciple is a learner.*

In the New Testament the word "disciple" is used broadly to describe the followers of a variety of leaders: the followers of Moses in John 9:28, of the Pharisees in Matthew 22:15, of John the Baptist in Matthew 9:4, and of Jesus in Matthew 10:1.

Though the word "disciple" occurs 250 times in the Scriptures, it is used only once in the Old Testament. It is used many times in the Gospels, sparingly in the book of the Acts, and not at all in the Epistles. In fact, after the day of Pentecost, which is recorded in Acts 2, the words used for the concept of disciple are "brethren," "beloved," "fellow-laborer," or "saint."

Thus, after Pentecost it seems that the word used for disciple is one which would more accurately convey the thought of the community of believers, the common life of the New Christians.

There is a progressive development in the meaning of discipleship which runs through the whole New Testament. A major change seems to take place on the day of Pentecost. Though all believers before and after Pentecost were saved, it is only those believers after Pentecost who were indwelt by the Holy Spirit. At Pentecost, we learn that conversion is made a part of discipleship, and from that point on the word "disciple" is rarely used.

In this book we will look at people in four spiritual contexts: the convert, the disciple, the disciplemaker, and the maker of disciplemakers.

We will now investigate the qualifications for being a disciple.

The Bible lists certain qualifications for disciples. I believe there are at least ten:

1. A disciple must be born again.
2. A disciple loves God.
3. A disciple is a learner.
4. A disciple is under Christ's authority.
5. A disciple abides in the Word of God.
6. A disciple loves the household of faith.
7. A disciple bears fruit.
8. A disciple must be willing to forsake people.
9. A disciple positively identifies with Christ.
10. A disciple must be willing to forsake possessions.

A disciple must be born again

The apostle John records that "Jesus replied, 'With all the earnestness I possess I tell you this: Unless you are born again, you can never get into the Kingdom of God'" (John 3:3 LB).

Within ourselves we have no desire or ability to be a disciple of Jesus Christ. This moving is a supernatural work of the power of God. We cannot have that work happening within us apart from a vital and dynamic relationship with Him. This begins at the point of conversion. "For apart from me you can't do a thing" (John 15:5 LB).

Some people have the mistaken idea that conversion is to be the end of the Christian life. The fact is that conversion is merely the beginning. Beyond the threshold of the conversion experience lies an entire lifetime of growing in the grace and knowledge of Jesus Christ.

A *disciple loves God*

Jesus summed it up: "But when the Pharisees had heard that he had put the Sadducees to silence, they were gathered together. Then one of them, which was a lawyer, asked him a question, tempting him, and saying, Master, which is the great commandment in the law? Jesus said unto him, Thou shalt love the Lord thy God with all thy heart, and with all thy soul, and with all thy mind. This is the first and great commandment. And the second is like unto it, Thou shalt love thy neighbour as thyself. On these two commandments hang all the law and the prophets" (Matt. 22:34–40). A disciple loves God with all his being.

A *disciple is a learner*

A learner has a learner's attitude. It matters not how much or how little one knows; the key is whether or not one is trying to learn ... whether or not one has the attitude of a learner.

A learner is a humble person. Paul says, "As your spiritual teacher, I give this piece of advice to each one of you. Don't cherish exaggerated ideas of your self or your importance, but try to have a sane estimate of your capabilities by the light of the faith that God has given to you all" (Rom. 12:3, Phillips). This verse teaches that two things can be sinful: a feeling that one is overly important; and a feeling that one can't do anything. The proper balance is to have a sane estimate of one's capabilities.

God has created us with certain talents and abilities. When He re-created us in Jesus Christ, at the time of our conversion, the experience of being born again, He gave us certain spiritual gifts. But if we try to operate beyond the dimensions of what God has provided for us, we are wasting our time. That is why it is imperative that we have a "sane estimate of (our) capabilities."

A learner is a teachable person. Solomon says, "The wise man is glad to be instructed, but a self-sufficient fool falls flat on his face" (Prov. 10:8 LB). Later in the same chapter in verse 17, he says, "Anyone willing to be corrected is on the pathway to life. Anyone refusing has lost his chance" (Prov. 10:17 LB).

In Proverbs 12:1 *(Good News Bible)* he says, "Anyone who loves knowledge wants to be told when he is wrong. It is stupid to hate being corrected." A person who loves knowledge wants to be told when he/she is wrong. The other side of the coin is Proverbs 9:8, "Never correct a conceited man; he will hate you for it. But if you correct a wise man, he will respect you" *(Good News Bible).*

A learner is hungry. In Nehemiah 9:3 (MLB) the prophet says, "They stood in their places for a fourth part of the day, while the book of the Law of the Lord their God was being read and for another fourth part of it they made confession and worshiped the Lord their God." These people were so hungry for the Word of God that for a fourth of a day they stood and listened to it being read. That is six hours of continuous listening . . . while standing up! On a modern scale of time usage and comfort, such devotion is unimaginable. And because the Word of God is living, hearing that much of the Scriptures caused them to spend another six hours confessing their sins and worshiping God.

In Proverbs 27:7 the writer says, "The full soul loatheth an honeycomb; but to the hungry soul every bitter thing is sweet."

A learner doesn't act as if he knows it all. Paul describes him thus: "Work happily together. Don't try to act big. Don't try to get into the good graces of important people, but enjoy the company of ordinary folks. And don't think that you know it all" (Rom. 12:16 LB).

A *disciple is under Christ's authority*

"A disciple is not above his teacher, but everyone when he is fully taught will be like his teacher" (Luke 6:40 RSV). As Jesus was under the authority of His Father, so we must be under the authority of Jesus.

Before one is born again, he has no choice about who his master is. An unconverted man is under the dominion of Satan. This is evident in Acts 26:18 where it says that man must be delivered from the power of Satan.

An unconverted person possesses the sin nature. Paul says, ". . . seeing that ye have put off the old man with his deeds" (Col. 3:9). An unconverted person is trapped by the sin nature and cannot get out, except through Christ. When one is converted God does basically two works in that life: first, He separates the person from the sin nature; and, secondly, He gives the person a new nature. Paul asks, "What shall we say then? Shall we continue in sin, that grace may abound? God forbid. How shall we, that are dead to sin, live any longer therein?" (Rom. 6:1,2).

Death equals separation. "Sin" as used here speaks of the sin nature in all of us. These two verses are saying that we are separated from the sin nature when we accept Christ. Paul goes on, "Know ye not, that so many of us as were baptized into Jesus Christ were baptized into his death? Therefore we are buried with him by baptism into death: that like as Christ was raised up from the dead by the glory of the Father, even so we also should walk in newness of life" (Rom. 6:3,4). To walk means to live. And newness of life speaks of a new source . . . we have a new life source. We are separated from the control, or the power of the sin nature and we live in that new life source, which is Christ.

This means that within those who are converted there are basically two natures. They still have the sin nature, although it is not dominant or, at least it need not be. But they also now have a new nature which is the life of Christ Himself within them. The key to being a disciple or not is that we Christians have a choice as to which of these natures will have the preeminence or control in our lives. *We have the choice.* The converted person can make Christ his/her authority. We need to yield to His inner working by a continual act of the will.

The story is told of an old Indian chief who was converted. After he came back to the tribe, they watched him closely. One day the council asked the chief, "Chief, you say you have been converted to Christianity, and yet we do not see all of your old ways changing. Can you explain that to us?" The old chief replied, "Yes, I can explain. Since I have become a Christian, inside me there are two dogs. White dog say do good. Black dog say do bad. Which dog win depend on which dog me say sic 'em." We need to make the daily choice of yielding to Christ as our authority.

A *disciple abides in the Word of God*

To "abide" means to continue on a course entered upon . . . to draw from something which sustains life. It is to be likened to a plant. A plant abides in and continues to draw sustenance from the soil. It cannot live apart from the soil. And abiding can be likened to a fish. A fish must of necessity abide in the water to draw the oxygen to his gills to live. A fish cannot live out of water.

In the same way, Jesus said that we cannot bear fruit except we abide in Him: "I am the vine, ye are the branches: He that abideth in me, and I in him, the same bringeth forth much fruit: for without me you can do nothing" (John 15:5). Christ is the spiritual source in which we must abide . . . we do this abiding through obedience to His Word.

To reduce abiding to its least common denominator means simply to "obey." Whenever you read the word "abide" in the Bible, simply substitute the word "obey."

The disciple must have a continuing obedience.

To abide in the Word there are three things we must do: we must take it in, we must think it over, and we must live it out.

1. *We must take it in.* How? There are four basic ways. We can *hear* the Word of God preached. We can *read* it. We can *study* it. We can *memorize* it.

2. *We must think it over.* This is done by *meditation*. Meditation is chewing on what God has given us from His Word and digesting it. As we meditate we re-chew it and think about it, mulling it over again and again.

3. *We must live it out.* This is *application*, the crux of Christian living. A practical way to apply the Word is to ask certain questions when we are taking the Word in, and then to think it over. *One*, is there an example for me to follow? *Two*, is there a command for me to obey? *Three*, is there a sin to avoid? *Four*, is there a promise to claim? *Five*, is there a difficulty to explore? *Six*, is there something to pray over? *Seven*, are there new insights about God Himself?

But to truly abide in (obey) the Word of God, it is imperative that we recognize its authority. The two great attacks on authentic Christianity have always taken one of two routes. Critics either attack the work and person of Jesus Christ or they attack the authority and authenticity of the Bible. So what you believe about the Bible is of great importance in applying it to your life.

The Bible itself claims it is more than print and page: it claims to be a living thing. "For the word of God is quick, and powerful, and sharper than any two-edged sword, piercing even to the dividing asunder of soul and spirit, and of the joints and marrow, and is a discerner of the thoughts and intents of the heart" (Heb. 4:12).

The Bible itself claims to be the Word of God: "All scripture is given by inspiration of God and is profitable for doctrine, for reproof, for correction, for instruction in righteousness" (2 Tim. 3:16).

So the authority of the Word must be recognized and it must be obeyed if one is to truly abide in it. Isaiah says that God is going to look to the man who trembles at His Word (66:2). In John 14:21 Jesus equates loving Him with obeying Him. In Psalm 119:59,60 David made haste and did not delay to obey God's commands.

What are some of the results of abiding in the Word?

1. *Abiding in the Word gives an increasing knowledge of God Himself.* "And how can we be sure that we belong to him? By looking within ourselves: are we really trying to do what he wants us to? Someone may say, 'I am a Christian; I am on my way to heaven; I belong to Christ.' But if he doesn't do what Christ tells him to, he is a liar. But those who do what Christ tells them to will learn to love God more and more. That is the way to know whether or not you are a Christian" (1 John 2:3–5 LB). The key to knowing if you are a Christian is not whether you are perfectly obeying God—no one is perfect—but whether or not it is your heart's desire to try to obey Him every day in every way.

2. *Abiding is the key to spiritual multiplication.* "And the word of God increased; and the number of the disciples multiplied in Jerusalem greatly . . ." (Acts 6:7). There is a direct connection between an increasing of the Word and the multiplying of disciples.

3. *Abiding in the Word of God is the key to knowing the enemy.* The reason for this is that the devil is terribly consistent. He pulls the same kind of tricks all the time: "Lest Satan should get an advantage of us: for we are not ignorant of his devices" (2 Cor. 2:11). We are not ignorant of his devices because we have read in the Word of God all the tricks he has used—and he is still using the same old tricks. In dealing with Satan it gives us the advantage to know his methods . . . and we can know by abiding in the Bible, where they all are recorded. Paul says, "But I fear lest by any means as the serpent beguiled Eve through his subtlety so your mind should be corrupted

from the simplicity that is in Christ" (1 Cor. 11:3). Bank tellers do not learn to recognize counterfeit money by examining counterfeit money. They concentrate on the real article for such an extended period of time, that whenever anything shows up which is not real, to them it is obviously counterfeit. The same is true with us. If we abide in the Word of God and know what the real article is, whenever the devil runs in a counterfeit, it sticks out like a sore thumb. Abiding in the Word is a key to knowing and recognizing the enemy.

A disciple loves the household of faith

"A new command I give unto you, That ye love one another; as I have loved you, that ye also love one another. By this shall all men know that ye are my disciples, if ye have love one to another" (John 13:34,35). We are commanded to love one another; there is no option. It is a central "must" for the Christian disciple.

One of the marks of loving others is being a servant to the body of Christ. Jesus says, "For even the Son of man came not to be ministered unto, but to minister, and to give his life a ransom for many" (Mark 10:45). In Luke 22:27 Jesus says, "For whether is greater, he that sitteth at meat, or he that serveth? is not he that sitteth at meat? but I am among you as he that serveth."

Paul has the same message: "For we preach not ourselves, but Christ Jesus the Lord; and ourselves your servants for Jesus' sake" (2 Cor. 4:5). But the teaching of the servanthood of the believer is not just in the New Testament. It runs through the whole Bible, as evidenced in Isaiah 43:10, "Ye are my witnesses saith the Lord, and my servant whom I have chosen. . . ."

Another mark of love for the brethren is a unifying spirit. Paul says, "As God's prisoner, then, I beg you to live lives worthy of your high calling. Accept life with humility and patience, making allowances for each other because you love each other. Make it your aim to be at one in the Spirit, and you will inevitably be at peace with one another" (Eph. 4:1–3 Phillips). When we are one in the Spirit we *will* be at peace with one another. F. F. Bruce in his Expanded Paraphrase translates 1 Corinthians 12:25, "that there be no division in the body, no sense of superiority or inferiority in the parts of the body." God doesn't desire that we have either a superiority or inferiority complex. He simply wants us to have a unifying spirit. He doesn't want divisiveness in the body of Christian believers. In John 17, (the high priestly prayer of Jesus). He prayed for the unity of believers, asking God: "That they all may be one; as thou, Father, art in me, and I in thee, that they also may be one in us: that the world may believe that thou hast sent me" (v. 21).

Love for fellow Christians is not an emotion, any more than love for God is an emotion; it is a direct act of the will. John says, "In this the children of God are manifest, and the children of the devil: whosoever doeth not righteousness is not of God, neither he that loveth not his brother" (1 John 3:10). In other words, John is explaining that the way one can tell who belongs to God and who belongs to the devil is by looking at their lives: "Whosoever doeth not righteousness is not of God. Neither he that loveth not his brother."

It is one thing to keep from sinning—this is the negative aspect. It is quite another thing to *do* righteousness. That is a positive act. The ultimate measure is not whether we are simply keeping from sinning, but whether or not we are making a positive outreach in righteousness. And the same is true of love: " . . . neither he that loveth not his brother." It doesn't say "he who does not hate his brother"—that would be the negative aspect. It says he who "loveth not his brother"—speaking of the positive, the outreaching aspect. It must be a positive outreach, not simply a negative lack of hate.

And, incidentally, this fulfills the law of God. Paul says, "Love does no wrong to anyone. That's why it fully satisfies all of God's requirements. It is the only law you need" (Rom. 13:10 LB). Therefore, if in your disciplemaking ministry, whether you are helping someone else or if you are getting help yourself, if what you are doing does not eventuate in love, then it is not of God. Paul says, "The object of all instruction is to call forth that love which comes from a pure heart, a clear conscience, and a sincere faith" (1 Tim. 1:5, 20th Century New Testament.)

The Bible also admonishes us to love our neighbors. This is related in the story of the Good Samaritan in Matthew 19. We are also commanded to love our enemies (Matt. 5:44).

The greatest treatise on love in the Bible, and perhaps in all of literature, is 1 Corinthians 13. Let me summarize it: we express our love by being patient and kind, loyal (no matter what it costs), by not being jealous, boastful, proud, haughty, glad about injustice, selfish, rude, irritable, or touchy. We also exhibit love by rejoicing whenever truth wins out, by always believing in others, expecting the best of others, always standing our ground in defending others, and by not holding grudges, hardly even noticing when others do us wrong.

John says, "My children, let us love not merely in theory or in words—let us love in sincerity and in practice! If we live like this, we shall know that we are children of the truth and can reassure ourselves in the sight of God, even if our own hearts make us feel guilty. For God is infinitely greater than our hearts, and he knows everything" (1 John 3:18–20 Phillips). Love is a positive, active verb.

A *disciple must bear fruit*

"Herein is my Father glorified, that ye bear much fruit; so shall ye be my disciples" (John 15:8).

Fruit is the outward manifestation of God's inner working. It is the invisible working of God in a person's life, gradually producing godlike character. Its outward manifestation is revealed in good works, . . . in reaching people for Christ (see Prov. 11:30), and in giving. But perhaps the greatest dividend is seen in the development of godlike character. The natural overflow of this god-likeness will reach out to others. The inward godlike character is described in Galatians 5:22,23 as "love, joy, peace, longsuffering, gentleness, goodness, faith, meek-ness, temperance."

One of these characteristics, longsuffering, is of ines-timable importance. In 2 Timothy 2 there are 42 action verbs, and 32 of them have to do with endurance. Nothing in the world can take the place of persistence. Talent will not. Nothing is more common than unsuccessful men with talent. Genius will not. Unrewarded genius is al-most a proverb. Education will not. The world is full of educated derelicts. Persistence and determination alone are worthy goals. Press on! It is always too soon to quit!

Another tremendously significant "fruit of the spirit" is faith. There are three aspects of faith pointed out in 2 Corinthians 1:10, "Who delivered us from so great a death, and doth deliver: in whom we trust that he will yet deliver us. . . ." The three aspects of faith shown here are past, present, and future. The past faith is the faith we exercised when we received Jesus Christ as our Lord and Savior. Future faith—the "will yet deliver us"—is the faith to know we are going to be with Him in heaven. But the difficult one is the middle one, present faith—"doth deliver us." This means *today*. Our faith should be opera-tional today. It is the Colossians 2:6 type of faith, "And now just as you trusted Christ to save you, trust him, too, for each day's problems; live in vital union with him" (LB). You received Him by faith; walk daily in him in faith. This is one of the real marks of Christian growth.

Please note an interesting fact: when the apostle Paul left the church in Thessalonica and became concerned for them, he asked about their faith: In 1 Thessalonians 3:5, it says, "For this cause, when I could no longer forbear, I sent to know your faith, lest by some means the tempter have tempted you, and our labour be in vain" (1 Thess. 3:5). He didn't write back about their quiet time, Scripture memorization, Bible study, or outreach—but about their faith. Of course, the above listed actions could be stimulators to, or outgrowths of, their faith. But Paul emphasized *faith*. He said, "I sent to know your faith."

If you want to measure your spiritual growth, ask yourself this question: "Am I trusting God for more today than I was a year ago?" If you are, you have probably grown. If not, you are probably static and stagnant.

A *disciple must be willing to forsake people*

Jesus says, "If any man come to me, and hate not his father, and mother, and wife, and children, and brethren, and sisters, yea, and his own life also, he cannot be my disciple" (Luke 14:26).

A young man came to me one day confessing that he was having some real troubles with what he called "inconsistencies" in the Bible. They were causing him bitterness. One of them was this verse in Luke. I believe the word "hate" is poorly translated from the Greek. What the Greek word means is "he who does not prize less highly." It doesn't mean you must hate your parents or others; that would obviously be unscriptural. It does mean that if you are confronted with a choice on some spiritual decision, Jesus and His Word must come first.

A *disciple must positively identify with Christ*

Jesus should also be first as far as identification is concerned. Are you willing to be identified with Him? Jesus says, "And whosoever doth not bear his cross, and come after me, cannot be my disciple" (Luke 14:27).

The Bible clearly teaches that the Christian will have problems if he identifies with Christ. This isn't just a statement; it is a promise. Paul says, "Yea, and all that will live godly in Christ Jesus shall suffer persecution" (2

Tim. 3:12). Paul suffered persecution. He once said, "And I, brethren, if I yet preach circumcision, why do I yet suffer persecution? then is the offense of the cross ceased" (Gal. 5:11). Jesus said, "These things I have spoken unto you, that in me ye might have peace. In the world ye shall have tribulation; but be of good cheer; I have overcome the world" (John 16:33). Expect tribulation if you live for Him.

A *disciple must forsake possessions*

In Luke 14:33 Jesus says, "So likewise, whosoever he be of you that forsaketh not all that he hath, he cannot be my disciple."

This can be a monumental problem to many. If there is anything in your life that you hold on to and would not surrender to God, then discipleship is out of the question. Jesus said it plainly in Mark 4:19, "And the cares of this world, and the deceitfulness of riches, and the lusts of other things entering in, choke the word, and it becometh unfruitful."

So, a disciple is all these things we have discussed. He must be born again and a learner. He loves God, is under Christ's authority, abides in the Word, loves other Christians, bears fruit, is willing to forsake people, makes a positive identification with Christ, and is willing to forsake possessions.

How are you doing in your journey toward discipleship? Some feel that they cannot "make it" if they must explicitly obey all of these "marks of a disciple." This isn't true, for there are degrees of discipleship. If all ten of these marks are not present in your life now, they certainly can be. No one can consistently have all these marks in his life every moment . . . this will not be true until we meet Jesus face to face and see Him as He is and become like Him. So don't become discouraged. Let's not forget Joel 2:25 where God says, "And I will restore to you the years that the locust hath eaten. . . ." Only God can do that. If you have wasted some years of your Christian life, (and I certainly have), this verse should give you great comfort. This verse shows the work of the sovereign grace, mercy, goodness, and love of God. Don't be discouraged. It doesn't make any difference how far you've gone; the love of God in Christ goes one step further. Not only can He use you; but He wants to use you.

As a help to you if your desire is to go further with Christ, or if you're wanting to help someone else, the following is a suggested list on basic follow-up. You'll find some principles and topics, some suggested projects to help with them, some suggested tapes to listen to, and books to read, as well as scriptures to consider. These can be a blessing to your own life, and they can also help you as you begin to work with others.

Basic Follow-Up Outline

The twenty-three principles listed below are certainly not exhaustive. Neither are they placed in the absolute order of importance in a Christian's life. However, they are, I believe, indicative of the direction that God would have us go. You will find listed the principle and then resources which may be of help in implementing or teaching the principle. The resources may be questions, project assignments, scriptures, tapes, books, or pamphlets. All of the tapes listed as resources are available on a free-loan basis for only postage and handling from the Discipleship Library, 435 West Boyd, Norman, Oklahoma 73069. A catalogue to the Discipleship Library costs $2.00. It currently includes over 7,000 messages.

1. *Assurance of Salvation.* The following scriptures will help in the area of believing and receiving: John 20: 28–31; 3:16; 3:36; 5:24; 6:37–40; 11:25,26; 1:12.

The following will help regarding assurance: Romans 8:38,39; 1 John 5:11–13; Jude 24,25; I Peter 1:3–5.

A resource tape: *Assurance* by Kenneth Chafin.

A helpful booklet: *Fact, Faith, and Feeling* by Billy Graham.

2. *The Devotional Life.* Psalm 27:7,8; 143:8; 5:3; 63:1,2; Mark 1:35; Luke 6:12,13, Proverbs 8:34 (LB).

Tapes available: *Quiet Time* by Warr.

Booklets available: *Quiet Time* by Inter-Varsity Christian Fellowship; *Manna in the Morning* by Stephen Olford; *My Heart—Christ's Home* by Robert Boyd Munger.

3. *The Authority of the Bible.* 2 Timothy 3:14–17; Hebrews 4:12; Jeremiah 23:29; 22:5.

1. Read Psalm 119 and list what the Word can do for you and what you are to do with the Word of God.

2. What is the Word of God from these verses: Ephesians 6:17; John 12:48; 17:17; Luke 21:33; John 6:63, Luke 8:11; Isaiah 55:11?

3. From the following verses, summarize the value of the Word of God in a believer's life: Matthew 4:4; Isaiah 55:11; Hebrews 4:12; Psalm 119:105; John 5:39, 2 Timothy 3:4–17; Psalm 119:9,11; Numbers 15:39; John 15:3; 1 Peter 2:2.

4. From 2 Timothy 3:16, identify and define each thing the Word is profitable for.

Tapes available: *Authority and Sufficiency of the Word* by Lorne Sanny; *The Word of God* by Max Barnett: *The Authority of the Scriptures* by Jack Mayhall; *Why the Bible?* by Gene Warr.

Available books: *Evidence That Demands a Verdict* by Josh McDowell; *The Authority of the Bible* by John Stott.

4. *How to Take in the Word of God* (The hand illustration by the Navigators). This has to do with hearing, reading, studying, memorizing, and meditating on the Word of God. A complete explanation is available from The Navigators, P. O. Box 20, Colorado Springs, CO 80901. Tapes are also available from the discipleship library on the hand illustration given by a number of good people.

5. *The Balanced Christian Life* (The wheel illustration). A complete explanation is available from The Navigators, P.O. Box 20, Colorado Springs, CO 80901. The wheel has Jesus Christ at the center. The rim of the wheel represents the obedient Christian living the life. The four spokes of the wheel are the Word of God, prayer, fellowship, and witnessing.

Tapes available: *The Christ-centered Life* by Larry Woods; *The Wheel* by Gene Warr.

6. *How to Pray.*

1. List the principles of prayer from the prayer life of Jesus in the Gospels and write a personal "When I need to pray" application for each principle.

2. As you read through the Psalms, keep a list of when David cried to God and why. Then categorize the reasons and write a personal application for each category.

3. Read the first chapter of Paul's letters, plus Ephesians 3. List all the specific things Paul prayed for believers. Beside each specific prayer request put the name of a believer. Pray for that particular person during the coming week.

4. Memorize and meditate on 1 John 5:14,15.

5. Set up a time each week to pray with another Christian.

Tapes available: *Prayer* by Jim Peterson; *Prayer* by Peter Lord; *What Is Intercessory Prayer* and *How to Pray for the Lost?* by Barry Wood; *Prayer* by Larry Woods; *Prayer* by George Sanchez.

Books and booklets available: *Ministry of Intercession* by Andrew Murray; *Praying Hyde* by Francis McGaw; *George Mueller of Bristol* by Arthur T. Pierson; *Power through Prayer* by E. M. Bounds; *Rheer Howell—Intercessor* by Norman Grubb; *How to Spend a Day in Prayer* by Lorne Sanny; *With Christ in the School of Prayer* by Andrew Murray; *Prayer: Conversing with God* by Rosalind Rinker.

7. *How to Meditate on Scripture.* Tapes available: *Meditation* by Bill Gothard; *Control of Our Thoughts* by Stephen Olford.

Books available: *Primer of Meditation* by Jim Downing.

8. *Financial Responsibility.* The four basic areas of financial responsibility are earning, saving, spending, and giving money. Matthew 6:19,20.

Tapes available: *Financial Responsibility* by Gene Warr; *Work* by Max Barnett.

Books available: *You Can Be Financially Free* by George Fooshee; *God's Miraculous Plan of Economy* by Jack Taylor.

For a study on giving, the following will be helpful:

1. From 2 Corinthians 8 & 9, Philippians 4:10–20, and Luke 6:38 list the principles of giving.

2. From Galatians 6:6 and 2 Corinthians 9:6–15 list at least five areas where we should give.

3. List how we are to give from these verses: Deuteronomy 16:17; Deuteronomy 8:18; 2 Corinthians 9:7–14; Matthew 10:8; Proverbs 3:9,10; 1 Corinthians 16:2.

4. List the characteristics and consequences of Ananias's and Sapphira's giving program in Acts 5:1–10.

9. *How to Resist Satan.* James 4:7–8; Ephesians 6:10–20.

1. From Genesis 3:1–6, list the steps Satan used in tempting Eve.

2. From James 1:13–15, who tempts us? List the steps we follow in surrendering to temptation.

3. From 1 John 2:15–17, what areas does Satan appeal to in tempting us? Define each area. Correlate each area from 1 John 2:15–17 with Jesus' temptation in Matthew 4:1–10.

4. Read Matthew 4:1–10. List how Jesus dealt with temptation and list two areas in which you face temptations.

5. Meditate on James 4:7,8; 1 Corinthians 10:13; Hebrews 12:3,4; Revelation 12:11.

Tapes available: *James 1* by Peter Lord; *Drives* by Peter Lord; *Conflict with Sin and Trials and Temptation* by Larry Woods.

10. *How to Walk in the Spirit.* Galatians 5:16,17.

1. Study the following Scripture passages to prepare yourself for walking in the Spirit.

a. What does God command in this area? See 1 Thessalonians 4:4.

b. What should I know about Satan's attack in this area? See 1 Corinthians 10:13.

c. What can I do in regard to my will to walk in the Spirit? Job 31:1.

d. What main defensive weapon can I use? 1 Timothy 6:17.

e. What principles do we find on walking in the Spirit from David's prayer for purity? Psalm 119:35–37.

f. How does associating with godly people help me to walk in the Spirit? Proverbs 27:17; 13:20.

g. How can I avoid some of Satan's traps? Proverbs 4:25–27.

2. In studying how to stand fast in the trial of fire which would tempt us to walk in the flesh:

a. Who did Christ immediately identify with when the adulterous woman walked up? John 8:6–10.

b. When possible, what is better than fighting temptation? 2 Timothy 2:22; Genesis 39:12.

c. What weapon did Christ use in temptation? Matthew 4:3–11.

3. From the following verses, give reasons for walking in the Spirit and living a holy life: Psalm 24:3–4, 1 Peter 1:22.

Tapes available: *Purpose* by Peter Lord; *The Kind of a Woman God Wants* by Leila Sparks; *Knowing God* (Tape 1, 2, and 3) by Peter Lord; *The Perfect Heart* by Diane

Sargent; *Becoming a Whole Person* by Tom Nesbitt; and *The Tabernacle* (Tapes 1–7) by Paul Burleson.

Books Available: *Called unto Holiness* by Ruth Paxon; and *Joni* by Joni Eareckson.

Also available is Transferable Concept #4 from Campus Crusade for Christ.

11. *How to Experience God's Love and Forgiveness* (and your own self-acceptance). 1 John 1:9; Luke 7:47.

    1. From Exodus 20:1–17, James 4:17–23, Romans 14:21–23, define sin.

    2. From the following verses, list the consequences of unconfessed sin and the results of confessing sin: Psalm 51; 79:9; Luke 7:47; Psalm 24:3-5; 66:18; John 15:7; Romans 4:7,8; 2 Chronicles 16:9; Hebrews 10:2; 10:17,18; 2 Corinthians 5:15; Isaiah 59:1,2; 1 Kings 8:33,34; Psalm 32:1,2; 130:4; Colossians 2:13,14; Romans 6:10–14; Romans 6:10–12; 1 John 3:6; 2 Corinthians 6:16.

    3. From the following verses, list how one gains God's forgiveness: Acts 10:43; Mark 2:5; Matthew 26:28; John 6:53–55; Psalm 19:12; 139:23,24; 51:3,4; Genesis 39:9; 1 John 1:9; Psalm 32:5; Proverbs 28:13; Psalm 51:1; Mark 2:7; Lamentations 3:22,23; Psalm 78:38; 2 Chronicles 7:14; Psalm 51:10; 2 Chronicles 7:8–10; Matthew 6:14,15, and Luke 6:37.

    4. Visualize Micah 7:19 and Psalm 103:12 when confessing sin. Then visualize the blood of Jesus from the cross cleansing you as you confess your sin. Right down insights you gain during this time.

Tapes available: *Forgiveness* by Larry Christenson; and *Conflicts with Sin* by Larry Woods.

Forgiveness and self-acceptance are inevitably tied together. The following may be of help in the area of self-acceptance:

    1. Study Psalm 139 for insights into why you can accept yourself.

    2. From the following verses, answer the question,

"Who am I?" Psalm 139:13–16; John 1:12; Romans 8:16,17; 2 Corinthians 5:17; 1 Peter 2:9; 2 Corinthians 5:20.

3. From Isaiah 43:1–10, list "What God thinks of me."

4. Meditate on Romans 12:3 and from the following verses, write down why it is not wrong to love or accept yourself: Matthew 22:39; Leviticus 19:18; Mark 12:31; Romans 13:9,10; Galatians 5:14; and James 2:8.

5. Write down the names of people who have verbally told you, "I love you." Write down the names of people who have shown love to you and what the act of love was.

Books available: *Please Don't Hurt Me* by Leonard Keene; *Please Love Me* by Keith Miller.

12. *Living by Faith*. 1 Timothy 1:5; Romans 14:23; Hebrews 11:6.

1. Read Matthew 8:8,9 and 21:21. Underline the word <u>faith</u> wherever it appears. Why did Jesus perform these miracles? How can this increase our faith today?

2. Read Romans 4 and Genesis 12–22.

    a. On what was Abraham's faith based?

    b. Did he ever doubt?

    c. In what ways did he walk by sight?

    d. How did his faith grow?

3. List the things we depend upon God for by faith from these verses: John 3:16; Galatians 2:16; John 7:38, John 14:1; Ephesians 3:12–17; Acts 16:31; Galatians 2:20.

4. Read Proverbs 3:5,6.

    a. Define the meaning of all the verbs in these verses.

    b. Write out those verses using first person singular.

    c. What does "with *all* your heart" mean to you?

    d. Why can you trust God with all your heart?

    e. List areas of your life where you haven't been

trusting God and how you can acknowledge Him in those areas.

 f. How can you help a new Christian develop faith in God?

 5. Read Hebrews 11:1–31 and list how each person demonstrated faith. Read Hebrews 11:32–40 and list how each person demonstrated faith.

 6. Matthew 6:25–33.

  a. What does God promise He will provide?

  b. What are we to seek?

  c. What is His kingdom?

  d. What is His righteousness?

  e. What steps can we take to trust Him more for what He's promised to provide?

  f. What can we do to seek His kingdom and righteousness?

 7. From the following verses, how are we to grow in faith? Hebrews 11:6; Luke 7:1–10; Romans 10:17.

 8. From James 2:14–26, define in detail the relationship between faith and works.

Tapes available: *Faith* by Ruth Myers; *How God Provided Finances for Our New Building* by Hal Brooks; *Giving* by Russ Johnston.

Books available: *They Found the Secret* by V. Raymond Edman; *Shadow of the Almighty* by Elisabeth Elliot; *God Can Make It Happen* by Russ Johnston.

13. *How to Develop a Servant Heart.*

 I. *Develop humility.* Matthew 10:24; 20:28; Luke 17:7–10; 1 Peter 2:18; Philippians 2:3–8; Mark 10:45; Luke 22:26,27; Romans 12:16 (LB); Philippians 2:19–22; 2:25–30; Acts 20:19.

  1. Study the life of Ziba. 2 Samuel 9:2,11; 16:1–4; 19:24–27.

  2. From Deuteronomy 15, list the rights, privileges, and duties of a bondslave; then read Luke 17:7–10 and make a personal application.

3. From the following verses, list the characteristics of a humble life and pick out one weak area in your life and develop a project to help in that area. 1 Peter 2:18; Philippians 2:3–8; Luke 22:26,27; Romans 12:16; Philippians 2:19–22; Philippians 2:25–30; Acts 20:19; Mark 10:45.

4. Meditate on James 4:6 and why that is true.

5. From meditation on these verses, make two columns: "My part in becoming a success" and "God's part in making me a success." 1 Peter 5:5,6; Psalm 75:6,7; Matthew 20:16; Isaiah 66:2.

II. *Learn to Meet Practical Needs of Others*

1. Physical. Matthew 25:35–40; Matthew 10:42; Romans 12:13–15; 1 Peter 4:9; Hebrews 13:1–3; Hebrews 6:10.

a. Commit yourself to learn from one who is already proficient at serving others.

b. List the practical needs of those you are in contact with every day and list at least one way you can meet that need.

2. Spiritual.

a. Read 1 Thessalonians 1 and 2 and list what the Thessalonians' needs were and how Paul met them.

b. Repeat the above project with Ephesians 1, Colossians 1, and Philippians 1.

Tapes available: *Becoming a Disciplemaker* (Tapes 1–4) by Gene Warr; *How to Train a Disciple* by Walt Henrichsen; *Developing Disciplemakers* and *Objectives in Making Disciples* by LeRoy Eims; *Concept and Philosophy of Disciplemaking* by Skip Gray; *The Difference Between Help and Training* by Dave Dawson; *Ministry, Philosophy, and Strategy* by Max Barnett; *Follow Me Principle* by Max Barnett; *Making Disciples* by Doug Sparks; *Building* (Tapes 1–4) by Doug Sparks; *Building into Another's Life* by Leila Sparks; *Qualities Needed for Helping Others and Recruiting Girls to the Great Com-*

mission by Jodi Baker; *Discipleship Principles I, II, and III* and *Training I and II* by Larry Woods.

Books available: *Conserving the Fruits of Evangelism* by Dawson Trotman; *The Dynamics of Personal Follow-up* by Gary Kuhne; *Disciples Are Made, Not Born* by Walt Henrichsen; *Master Plan of Evangelism* by Robert Coleman; *How Jesus Trained Leaders* by Maxfield Garrett; *New Testament Follow-Up* by Waylon Moore; *What Made You Cross?* by J. H. Horsburgh.

14. *Openly Identifying with Christ.* Mark 8:34; Mark 8:38; Luke 14:27.

I. Study Acts 22 and Acts 26 listing the four areas of Paul's life covered in his testimony.

II. Using the outline from # I, write your own testimony.

III. From John 4:7–27, answer:

a. Why did the disciples marvel?

b. List principles Jesus used to communicate the gospel.

c. Write down why you think the Samaritan woman responded as she did.

IV. From 1 Peter 3:15, 1 John 1:3, and John 9:24,25, write down what you think the value of your testimony is.

V. From the following verses, list the condition and future of the unbeliever and your responsibility as a Christian: Ezekiel 3:18–19; 1 Timothy 2:4; Acts 1:8; 2:1–24; 2:32–47; Luke 16:27,28; 2 Thessalonians 1:7–10; Acts 18:6; 24:14–16; 3:12–20; Revelation 20:15; Romans 10:13–14; 1:14; Ezekiel 33:11; Mark 16:15; Acts 4:1–31; 8:1–5; John 3:36.

Tapes available: *Evangelism* by Billy Graham; *Students' Questions* by Paul Little, *The Great Resurrection Hoax* and *Nine-point Whammy* by Josh McDowell; *Enemies of Evangelism* by Skip Gray; *Importance of Evangelism* by Max Barnett; *Witnessing* by Pat Shaughnessy; *The Testimony* by Scott Smith.

Suggested books: *How to Give Away Your Faith* by Paul Little; *Winning Ways* by LeRoy Eims; *How to Witness* by Lorne Sanny.

15. *How to Reproduce Spiritually.* 2 Timothy 2:2. The example of Moses and Joshua, Elijah and Elisha, Jesus and the Twelve, Paul and Timothy.

For suggested tapes and books, see the spiritual section under #13, How to Develop a Servant Heart.

16. *How to Build a Christian Home.* Ephesians 5:25–27.

Tapes available: *Scriptural Home Seminar* by George Sanchez available from The Navigators; *Husband and Wife Relationship* by Jack and Carol Mayhall; *The Role and Responsibility of the Husband* by Gene Warr; *The Role and Responsibility of the Wife* by Irma Warr.

Books available: *Heaven Help the Home* by Howard Hendricks; *Letters to Philip* by Charlie Shedd; *Letters to Karen* by Charlie Shedd; *Do Yourself a Favor—Love Your Wife,* by H. Page Williams; *Me Obey Him,* by Elizabeth Rice Handford; *The Total Woman* by Marabel Morgan; *Children—Fun or Frenzy?* by Al and Pat Fabrizio.

17. *Priorities and the Use of Time.* Ephesians 5:15–17.

Tapes available: *Priorities and the Use of Time* by Max Barnett; *Priorities and the Use of Time* by Gene Warr; *How to Get Control of Your Time and Your Life* by Alan Lakein; *Managing Your Time* by Ted Engstrom.

Booklet available: *Tyranny of the Urgent* from IVCF.

18. *Vision.* To examine Jesus' vision and to gain perspective into what to give your life to.

Tapes available: *Vision* by Jim Peterson; *Born to Reproduce* by Dawson Trotman; *Possibilities of a Life* by Max Barnett; *Pacesetting* by John Crawford; *Spiritual Leadership* by Larry Woods.

Books available: *Master Plan of Evangelism* by Robert Coleman; *How Jesus Trained Leaders* by W. Maxfield Garrett.

19. *Lordship of Christ.* (Total commitment) Luke 6:46; Luke 14:33; John 13:13; Acts 2:36; Philippians 2:11;

1. Meditate on Luke 14:37–45.

2. Go through the Gospels listing the costs and rewards of making Christ Lord, according to Jesus.

3. Read Hebrews 11. List the price each person paid to be on God's honor roll.

4. Meditate on Mark 8:34–37 and Matthew 16:24–26.

5. From Romans 6,7, and 8, list the characteristics of the old and new natures, and how we are to overcome the old nature.

Tapes available: *Jesus Is Lord* by Gene Warr. *Authority of the Believer* by Jack Taylor; *Life Transforming Concepts I* by Tim Timmons; *What is the Christian Life?* and *How do I Live the Christian Life?* by Tim Timmons; *The Lordship of Christ* by Rod Sargent; *Total Commitment* by Helene Ashker; *Jesus Is Lord* by S. M. Lockridge.

Books and booklets recommended: *Have We No Rights?* by Maybelle Williamson; *My Heart—Christ's Home* by Robert Boyd Munger; *Calvary Road* by Roy Hession; *Continuous Revival* by Norman Grubb; *The Normal Christian Life* by Watchman Nee; *Saving Life of Christ* by W. Ian Thomas; *Where Is Your Treasure?* by William McDonald.

20. *Knowing God.* John 17:26; Psalm 69:36; 91:14; 31:23; Philippians 1:9.

1. Study the names of God out of a concordance, preferably Young's.

2. Study the seven major concepts of God: Loving, Holy, Forgiving, Heavenly Father, Unchanging, Provider, and Personal.

3. From John 17:26, study the life of Jesus and how He manifested the names of God to His disciples.

Tapes available: *Attributes of God* by Josh McDowell; *Names of God* by Jack Taylor; *Character of God's Nature I, II, III, IV* by Jim White; *Fellowship with God* by

George Sanchez; *Quiet Time* by Larry Woods; *Knowing God I, II, III* by Peter Lord.

Recommended books: *Knowing God* by J. I. Packer; *The Names of God* by Nathan Stone.

21. *Suffering.* Deuteronomy 13:3; James 1:12; Romans 5:3–5; Psalm 26:2,3; 1 Peter 4:12,13; 1:6; 2 Corinthians 1:3,4; 2 Timothy 3:12; John 16:33.

1. List the circumstances from your past and present for which you cannot understand the ways God was and is working.

2. Do a character study of Joseph.

3. Do a word study on prudence.

Tapes available: *Suffering* by Donald Grey Barnhouse; *Suffering* by Ruth Myers; *Trials and Temptations* by Larry Woods; *Trials* by Peter Lord; *Job Series I–V* by Gene Warr.

22. *Discovering God's Will.*

Recommended tapes: *The Will of God* by John Repass; *The Will of God* by Lorne Sanny.

23. *How to Study the Bible.* 2 Timothy 2:15.

1. From the following verses Ezra 7:10; Prov. 2:4; 2 Tim. 2:15) answer these questions:

a. What are the proper attitudes toward studying the Word?

b. Who are the people who studied the Word, and what was their occupation?

c. What is the objective of Bible study as opposed to other methods of intake of the Word?

d. What ways will Bible study benefit you that the other methods of intake of the Word will not?

e. Study Proverbs 2:1–10. List the attitudes to take in Bible study and the results of these attitudes.

Tapes available: *How to Gain Insights from Scripture* by Don Crossland; *Bible Methods I, II, III, IV, V* by Howard Hendricks.

Recommended book: *Joy of Discovery* by Oletta Wald.

3

Why Make Disciples?

If one is to devote a major part of his life to a cause, it is imperative that he be firmly convinced as to why he should do it. Making disciples should become part of the fiber of our doing and being, if for no other reason than simply to obey Christ's command to do it.

This chapter discusses the Great Commission, why I am committed to this means of ministry, and some misconceptions about the disciplemaking ministry.

The Great Commission

Here it is: "And Jesus came and said to them, 'All authority in heaven and on earth has been given to me. Go therefore and make disciples of all nations, baptizing them in the name of the Father and of the Son and of the Holy Spirit, teaching them to observe all that I have commanded you; and lo, I am with you always, to the close of the age' " (Matt. 28:18–20 RSV). This is a huge task, the biggest we will ever face on earth as men and women working for God. Jesus said He has been given "all authority" (the KJV says "all power"). We need that authority and power if we are to be the instruments in His hands for fulfilling the Great Commission.

The Great Commission has two basic parts. The first is *winning people to Christ.* Paul says in Acts 20:24, "But life is worth nothing unless I use it for doing the work assigned me by the Lord Jesus—the work of telling others

the Good News about God's mighty kindness and love"
(LB).

In Luke 19:10 Jesus says, "For the Son of man is come
to seek and to save that which was lost."

In 1 Timothy 2:4–6 Paul writes, "Who will have all men
to be saved, and to come unto the knowledge of the truth.
For there is one God, and one mediator between God and
men, the man Christ Jesus; who gave himself a ransom for
all, to be testified in due time."

And Peter points out, "The Lord is not slack concerning
his promise, as some men count slackness; but is longsuffering to us-ward, not willing that any should perish, but
that all should come to repentance" (2 Peter 3:9).

The second part of the Great Commission is *making
disciples.* Have you ever wondered why Christ commanded us to make disciples? Of all the tasks we could
possibly do on earth for Him, why should making disciples be so important? This is the concept this chapter will
explore.

First, it was Jesus' own method. In Mark 3:13–15 we
are told, "And he goeth up into a mountain, and calleth
unto him whom he would: and they came unto him. And
he ordained twelve, *that they should be with him,* and
that he might send them forth to preach, And to have
power to heal sicknesses, and to cast out devils. . . ."

He chose twelve *to be with him.* That is the principle—the "with him" principle. From that point on, although it is true that He also ministered to the multitudes,
He basically poured His life into these twelve, and, more
specifically, into three—Peter, James, and John.

In the first chapter of Acts when Jesus ascended to the
right hand of God the Father, in effect, He said to His
disciples, "I'm leaving the task with you." This meant it
was up to them to continue the spreading of Christianity
to the whole world, and their method was by making
disciples, who would make other disciples, who would
make . . . on and on.

Jesus spent much personal time with His followers: Mark 6:31 tells us, "And he said to them, 'Come away by yourselves to a lonely place, and rest a little while' " (RSV). Mark records, "Leaving that region they traveled through Galilee where he tried to avoid all publicity in order to spend more time with his disciples, teaching them" (9:30,31 LB).

Second, discipleship was Paul's method. Evidently Jesus personally trained him during Paul's "Arabia years." Then Paul, having learned his lessons well, turned right around and began making disciples of others. In fact, Paul had a sort of "traveling on the job training Bible school." In Acts 20:4 Luke says, "And there accompanied him into Asia Sopater of Berea; and of the Thessalonians, Aristarchus and Secundus; and Gaius of Derbe, and Timotheous; and of Asia, Tychicus and Trophimus."

If you follow the destinies of these men in the New Testament church you will see that they became elders, preachers, and church leaders all over Asia Minor.

Third, discipleship is the fastest way to fulfill the Great Commission. It employs the principle of multiplication, rather than addition.

One of the first commands God gave to man is "Be fruitful, and multiply, and replenish the earth" (Gen. 1:28). This was the quickest way to get the earth filled with people . . . and it is the quickest way to cover the earth with disciples.

Let's look at some examples of the power of multiplication: Suppose a man came to you, requesting a job. You ask him what salary he expects. He answers, "Start me with a penny the first day, then double my wages each day thereafter." You agree, thinking that a penny the first day, two cents the next, eight cents the fourth day, sixteen cents the fifth day . . . that is very cheap labor. So you hire him.

At the end of thirty-one days, he will have earned over

five million dollars. You have underestimated the power of multiplication and have lost a fortune. Looking at it from another viewpoint, the laborer did understand the power of multiplication and gained a fortune.

Another example of the power of multiplication over simple addition is for you to suppose that you could preach to 100,000 people each day. Supposing you have only a 4 percent response? You could reach 4,000 for Christ each day, or 1,460,000 per year. In 16 years you would have reached 23,360,000 people. That is the addition method.

But suppose you reach only one person and take six months to train that one. Then the two of you each reach and train another, then the four of you ... each time reproducing yourselves in six months. At the end of the same 16 years you would have reached over 4,000,000,000 people, which is just a little more than the present population of the earth.

Paul believed in the power of multiplication. In 2 Timothy 2:2 he says to Timothy, one of his key disciples, "And the things that thou hast heard of me among many witnesses, the same commit thou to faithful men, who shall be able to teach others also." Isaiah says, "Write down all these things I am going to do, says the Lord, and seal it up for the future. Entrust it to some godly man to pass on down to godly men of future generations" (8:16 LB). That is multiplication. Christ knew the infinite potential and the infinite worth of one individual. God says, "A little one shall become a thousand, and a small one a strong nation: I the Lord will hasten it in his time" (Isa. 60:22). See Ted's story in Chapter 1 for an example of this.

Fourth, it works. We have seen it in the biblical context. Disciples have been made over the centuries, and now there are representatives of Christianity in every nation on earth. Moses poured his life into Joshua; Elijah poured his life into Elisha; and on and on. Jesus to the

Twelve; the Twelve to others; Paul to Timothy; Timothy to faithful men; those faithful men to others also.

Why I am committed to this means of ministry

I am committed to it for three reasons: the brevity of life, a sense of stewardship, and a desire for my life to count for God.

First, *the brevity of life*. The Bible teaches that life is like a vapor. Swifter than a weaver's shuttle, it is like a tale that is told. It is fleeting like water poured out upon the ground which cannot be gathered up again. I can identify with David when he cried out in Psalm 71:9, "Cast me not off in the time of old age; forsake me not when my strength faileth." I understand that. And when David prayed in Psalm 71:18, "Now also when I am old and greyheaded, O God, forsake me not; until I have shewed thy strength unto this generation, and thy power to every one that is to come."

The only way I can show the power of God to "everyone who is to come" is by investing in the lives of people who will invest in the lives of other people who will invest . . . and that way, by the grace of God, I can show the power of God to generations yet to come.

There are even some promises regarding this: Isaiah 46:4 says, "Even to old age I am the same and to (the time of) gray hair I will bear you. I have made you and I will carry you: even I will bear you and save you " (MLB). Psalm 92:14 promises, "In old age they shall still be bearing fruit. They shall be full of life and vitality" (MLB).

Secondly, *a sense of stewardship*. We refer to life as "my life." It is precious. In Job 2:4 Satan says, ". . . all that a man hath will he give for his life." But why do we call it "*my* life?" I have a responsibility for the life that God has given me. I didn't manufacture it. I don't sustain it. It is something which God has loaned me for a short time while here on earth, and I believe I have a responsibility to invest it where it will count most. The psalmist says, "Let everyone bless God and sing his praises, for he holds our lives in his hands. And he holds our feet to the path" (Ps. 66:8,9 LB).

Thirdly, *I want my life to count for something worthwhile.* I'd hate to reach the end of the road and have it said of me as it was said of an old couple in Somerset Maugham's *Of Human Bondage:* "It was as if they had never lived at all." I don't want that to happen to me. I want to *live* and pass on abundant life in Christ to many, many others. I can do it through a ministry of spiritual multiplication, reproducing myself many times over in a disciplemaking ministry. And so can you.

Misconceptions in the ministry of multiplication

1. *That it is the only way to accomplish the Great Commission.* It is not either/or, but both/and. We are not only to disciple others, but we are to win others. After the resurrection Jesus appeared to Peter in John 21:15–17, and asked Peter if he loved Him. Peter said yes. In those three verses Jesus told Peter three times to "feed my lambs," "feed my sheep," "feed my sheep."

"Feeding sheep" means ministering to the multitude of the family of God. It is not the same thing as one-on-one discipleship. In Ephesians 4:11,12 Paul points out that God has given special gifts to some members of the body in order that they, the pastors/teachers, may develop the saints (the Christian community) to go out and do the ministry.

2. *That you have to be a finished product to help others become disciples.* You only have to be one step ahead of others to help them down the entire length of the road of life.

3. *That ministers can't do it because they are too busy.* They can do it, if they will pay the price.

4. *That you must be a minister to do it.* Sometimes even the ministers and theologians don't know how to

reach others face-to-face. Dr. W. A. Criswell tells the story of a group of modernistic theologians who met with the Lord Jesus. The Lord asked these famous and illustrious theologians, "Who do men say that I am?" And they replied, "Some say that you are John the Baptist raised from the dead; some say that you are Jeremiah or one of the prophets; and even some say you are the Christ, the Son of God." Then the Lord asked the theologians, "But who do *you* say I am?" And the theologians gave a learned answer, "Thou art the ground of being, thou art the leap of faith into the impenetrable unknown, thou art the existential, unphraseable, unverbalized, unpropositional confrontation with the infinitude of inherent, subjective experience." The Lord turned sadly away.

5. *That it is an unrealistic approach.* There is the story of the man who told Dwight Moody, the famous evangelist, that he didn't like his method of evangelism. Mr. Moody said he wasn't too happy with it himself, then asked the man what method he used. The man answered, "Oh, I don't have any method." Moody replied, "Well, I like mine better than yours."

True, if those who had begun the multiplication process thirty-two years ago would have succeeded with every convert and disciple, the entire world would have by now been totally reached for Christ. This is the reason quality is so important. Weak links in the chain do break the reproductive process. Every time you lose a link you cut your ultimate production in half. This is the reason I included in my philosophy of life the term, "qualified laborers."

6. *That you must see immediate, measurable results.* It took Jesus three years to train twelve people . . . and really only three in great depth. Why are *we* in such a hurry? In our society of "instantness" we want instant disciples. There is no such thing.

7. *That Paul was not trained.* If he weren't trained, he did a pretty good job of spreading Christianity across a

great segment of the world in his time! I believe he was trained in the Arabian desert under the personal tutelage of Jesus.

8. *That it will always succeed.* Obviously, it won't. There will always be weak links. The story of Gehazi, a disciple of Elisha in 2 Kings (5:15,16, 21–27), is a good example of this. Gehazi had every opportunity to learn. He saw Elisha heal the waters of the city which had produced barrenness; he saw bears attack the young men who had made fun of Elisha; he heard Elisha pray and saw God's answer as He filled ditches with water so that the men and animals could drink when fighting the Moabites; he saw the widow supplied supernaturally with enough oil to sell and pay off her debts and have sufficient remaining to live on; he saw the raising of the dead son of the Shulamite woman; he saw the poisoned pot of vegetables eaten by the sons of the prophets made pure by Elisha's throwing in a handful of meal; he saw Naaman the leper healed. And yet, in the end, Gehazi failed. One of the great misconceptions in working with people is that you always succeed. You don't.

My own stumbling efforts to make disciples certainly have not always been crowned with success. That's one of the things that breaks my heart. I remember a young man whom I will call Bill. After some seminary training Bill came to our city deeply disillusioned with Christianity and his own walk and life. As I began to meet, talk, and pray with him, I found that he knew nothing of the basic disciplines of the Christian walk. I shared these with him, and he responded positively to the idea. He began to meet the Lord morning by morning in a quiet time, began to memorize scripture, was effectively reaching out in witness to others, and was doing an excellent job of in-depth Bible study. He was capable of making a good living with his hands, which he was doing, when one day a small church in Oklahoma City called him to be their pastor. He accepted. The Lord blessed his ministry there, and we continued to fellowship. It wasn't long until a larger church in a distant state gave him a call, and he responded. In the larger situation, he was in a more affluent society. He began to drink socially, then steadily began to seek out the companionship of other women, and consequently lost his wife and family, and ended up a suicide in a motel. My heart yet yearns for him.

Then there was another whom I'll call George. George was a sharp fraternity man, socially very acceptable, a good businessman, and was seemingly sitting on top of the world. When he was about thirty years of age the claims of Christ were made clear to him for the first time, and he made that commitment. Then the roof fell in. He lost his job, moved to another city with his family, had difficulty finding employment, but finally, by the grace of God, was able to get a good job. He then began to move up in the economic scale again. He continued to walk with the Lord and encouraged others. But his desire for wealth began to shade his judgment, and he took a job which put him in compromising positions time and time again. Finally, the temptation was too great, and he succumbed. He left his wife and children. The last time I heard, he had married a widow older than himself, and was living on her money. George and I had spent literally hours together studying the Bible, praying together, going out on ministry assignments together. Often on my knees weeping in prayer, I wondered and asked God where I failed him.

Then let me tell you about a man whom I'll call Bill. Everyone liked Bill. He had a dear wife. They were active in their church, Sunday school, and home Bible study. For perhaps two years, they were about as faithful a couple as you could see. They grew and grew to a certain point, and then stopped—stagnated.

Today, Bill is relatively ineffective as a husband, as a father, and as a witnessing Christian. There were some issues in his life which he refused to deal with. One was submission to authority. He held on to a streak of rebelliousness. Secondly, unfaithfulness. Making promises and not keeping them. Starting jobs and not completing them. Thirdly, a refusal to operate with a margin. This was true with time as well as with money. Fourthly, a lack of wholeheartedness. Doing things as he wanted to do them or felt like it, instead of an all-out effort doing it as unto the Lord. Fifthly, just plain laziness, which in the final analysis is self-centeredness. Today, as I look at Bill, and recognize the infinite potential in his life, it grieves me to see him on the shelf outside the will of God.

These stories of failure are sobering. You ask me why I don't quit. The reason I don't, is because, thank God, there are other stories, too. After all this, if you're still interested, then your next question might be, "Well, where do I find a person to work with? What kind of a person do I look for? And what are the ground rules we play by?" We'll be covering that in the next chapter.

4

How to Make Disciples

Part I: Selecting Persons

Selecting people in any field of endeavor, whether it be corporate leadership, athletics, or the military, is a crucial process. Books have been written on how to hire, how to discover leadership potential, how to find the winner, and who will be successful. It is no less important in choosing people into whom you will pour your life so that they may become disciples. John 6 records that Jesus told the multitudes who followed him that if they did not eat his flesh and drink his blood, they could have no part in Him. Many, therefore, of his disciples said that it was a hard saying, and they went back, and walked no more with him. Then Jesus said to the twelve, "Will ye also go away?" Then Simon Peter answered him, "Lord, to whom shall we go? thou hast the words of eternal life. And we believe and are sure that thou art that Christ, the son of the living God" (John 6:68). That was commitment.

People will show interest who are simply curious. They'll say to themselves, "Isn't this interesting? I wonder what's going on here." And they'll come out of curiosity. Then if they listen long enough, they may become convinced. And their thought process goes like this: "I believe these people have it all figured out. Their heads are screwed on right. I better pay attention to what they're saying." But then in the final stage, when they move from simply being convinced to being committed, they will come and say in effect, "I want to throw in my lot with you. I want you to help me invest my life where it'll count for God. I want help in my Christian life, and I'm coming to you for it."

The starting point

You must be a disciple yourself. Isaiah says, "And the remnant that is escaped of the house of Judah shall again take root downward, and bear fruit upward . . ." (Isa. 37:31). That is always the key. The root must go down first before fruit will be borne upward. If you are to make disciples, you must *be* one.

Only God chooses the ones. Therefore, if you want to begin working with someone you should begin praying that God will reveal that one to you. Paul says, "This charge, son Timothy, I lay upon you, following that prophetic utterance which first pointed you out to me" (1 Tim. 1:18 NEB). God brought Paul and Timothy together.

God's selections may not be the ones we would make. Remember Samuel? He was looking for a man to be the king. The Bible says, "And it came to pass, when they were come, that he looked on Eliab, and said, Surely the Lord's anointed is before him. But the Lord said unto Samuel, Look not on his countenance, or on the height of his stature; because I have refused him: for the Lord seeth not as man seeth; for man looketh on the outward appearance, but the Lord looketh on the heart" (1 Sam. 16:6,7). Evidently Samuel had picked a tall, handsome man. But God selected the youngest and smallest of the lot, the boy who was out tending sheep. In 1 Samuel 16:12 God said, "Arise, anoint him: for this is he." This was quite a shock to Samuel, whose judgment had been shown to be in error, but he trusted God's choice. The result: David was a man after God's own heart.

Paul tells us we are all candidates, "For ye see your calling, brethren, how that not many wise men after the flesh, not many mighty, not many noble, are called: But God hath chosen the foolish things of the world to confound the wise; and God hath chosen the weak things of the world to confound the things which are mighty; And base things of the world, and things which are despised, hath God chosen, yea, and things which are not, to bring to nought things that are . . ." (1 Cor. 1:26–28).

We must be careful in selecting disciples because there are people who are great, but not good; there are people who are good, but not great; some are both good and great; and some are neither good nor great.

a. *People who are great, but not good.* We would have to admit that men like Napoleon, Hitler, and Stalin were great, but they certainly were not good.

b. *People who are good, but not great.* We should thank God for these people. They are the ones who always volunteer when something needs to be done. They are the ones who keep the local church running. They stay with it until the job is finished, although they get no recognition nor acclaim. This type of person moves quietly across the pages of the Bible, and where he/she walks you will find pleasant weather and companionship.

Such a person was Isaac, the son of a great father, and the father of a great son. He himself never rose above mediocrity.

Such a person was Boaz, the ancestor of King David.

Such people were Mary and Joseph, Mary's husband.

Such a person was Barnabas, the son of consolation.

Often people like this are not known beyond the borders of their own church fellowship, but their presence is a benediction wherever they go. When they die, they leave behind them a fragrance of Christ that lingers on long after the cheap celebrities of the day have been forgotten. I believe that's what John means in Revelation 14:13 where he says, "And I heard a voice from heaven saying unto me, Write, Blessed are the dead which die in the Lord from henceforth: Yea, saith the Spirit, that they may rest from their labours; and their works do follow them."

c. *People who are both good and great.* The greatest biblical example of this was Abraham.

d. *People who are neither good nor great.* Ahab, the

king of Israel, could have been one of these. Beneath his royal robes beats the heart of a weakling and coward. This whimpering, sulking fellow was a tool of Jezebel, his strong and wicked wife who corrupted him and ruined his people.

But the masses of people are not great; and the truth is that most of us are selfish, lustful, egotistical, opinionated, vain, and afraid. I don't think this is too harsh a judgment. Paul makes this same observation in Romans 3:9–19 and in Ephesians 2:1–3.

It is true that not all of us can be great, but by the grace of God and through Jesus Christ, we can all be good. But it takes time to know a person. You won't really know someone until you've spent considerable time with that person.

You need a "fishing pond." For years my fishing pond has been my Sunday school class and, also, my business associations.

It is interesting to note that the disciples went through three stages before they were really committed to Christ:

a. They were curious. This is graphically pointed out in John 1:35–59. The disciples initially followed Jesus because they wanted to hear what He had to say and to see what He would do. They listened and observed, but made no decision about what they heard or saw.

b. *They became convinced.* Matthew 16:13–16 reveals that after a period of time they became convinced about who He was. Peter gave the answer: "Thou art the Christ, the Son of the living God."

c. *They became committed.* Once they were convinced about His identity, Jesus pressed them for commitment. In John 8:31 Jesus says, ". . . If ye continue in my word, then are ye my disciples indeed." Jesus felt that those who believed in Him must abide in His Word if they were to be true disciples.

These three stages will be true of the men and women you find in any of the fishing ponds where God has put you. Watch for them.

Qualities to look for in a potential disciple

Availability

Isaiah was available. "Also I heard the voice of the Lord, saying, Whom shall I send, and who will go for us? Then said I, Here am I; send me" (6:8). What beautiful words to the Lord!

Ruth was available. Perhaps no lovelier words of availability have ever been written in all of literature: "And Ruth said, Intreat me not to leave thee, or to return from following after thee: for whither thou goest, I will go; and where thou lodgest, I will lodge: thy people shall be my people, and thy God my God: Where thou diest, will I die, and there will I be buried: the Lord do so to me, and more also, if ought but death part thee and me" (Ruth 1:16,17).

Elisha was available: "And Elijah said to Elisha, Tarry here, I pray thee; for the Lord hath sent me to Bethel. And Elisha said unto him, As the Lord liveth, and as thy soul liveth, I will not leave thee. So they went down to Bethel" (2 Kings 2:2).

Jonathan's armorbearer was available: "And Jonathan said to the young man that bare his armour, Come, and let us go over unto the garrison of these uncircumcised: it may be that the Lord will work for us: for there is no restraint to the Lord to save by many or by few. And his armourbearer said unto him, Do all that is in thine heart: turn thee; behold, I am with thee according to thy heart" (1 Sam. 14:6,7).

Pay close attention to the person who "keeps hanging around." Every time you turn around, you stumble over that one. Such a person is under your feet—available. And since you can't train those you don't have, begin training that one to be a disciple.

A heart for God

This is also what God is looking for. In Deuteronomy 5:29 God says, "O that there were such an heart in them, that they would fear me, and keep all my commandments always, that it might be well with them, and with their children for ever!" In 2 Chronicles 16:9 the writer tells us, "For the eyes of the Lord run to and fro throughout the whole earth to show himself strong in the behalf of them whose heart is perfect toward him" Psalm 53:2 (LB) states, "God looks down from heaven, searching among all mankind to see if there is a single one who does right and really seeks for God." And David says, "For the eyes of the Lord are intently watching all who live good lives, and he gives attention when they cry to him" (Ps. 34:15 LB).

A *love for people*

Of Jesus we are told:

The crowds were profoundly impressed by his answers—but not the Pharisees! When they heard that he had routed the Sadducees with his reply, they thought up a fresh question of their own to ask him. One of them, a lawyer, spoke up: "Sir, which is the most important command in the laws of Moses?" Jesus replied, " 'Love the Lord your God with all your heart, soul, and mind.' This is the first and greatest commandment. The second most important is similar: 'Love your neighbor as much as you love yourself.' All the other commandments and all the demands of the prophets stem from these two laws and are fulfilled if you obey them. Keep only these and you will find that you are obeying all the others." (Matt. 22:33–40 LB).

Far too many people today are like Charlie Brown who said, "I love the world. I think the world is wonderful. It's just people I can't stand."

Faithful

Daniel was faithful. "Then this Daniel was preferred above the presidents and princes, because an excellent spirit was in him; and the king thought to set him over the whole realm. Then the presidents and princes sought to find occasion against Daniel concerning the kingdom; but they could find none occasion nor fault; forasmuch as he was faithful, neither was there any error or fault found in him" (Dan. 6:3,4).

Abram was faithful. "Thou art the Lord the God, who

didst choose Abram, and broughtest him forth out of Ur of the Chaldees, and gavest him the name of Abraham; and foundest his heart faithful before thee . . ." (Neh. 9:7–8a).

In Luke 16:10 Jesus says, "He that is faithful in that which is least is faithful also in much: and he that is unjust in the least is unjust also in much."

Remember, as Solomon says in Proverbs 25:19, "Confidence in an unfaithful man in time of trouble is like a broken tooth, or a foot out of joint."

If I could select one attribute that would be the least common denominator for a disciple who will stick it out, it would be faithfulness.

| Basic ground rules for making disciples |

Recruit to Jesus and to the vision of the ministry—not to an organization or to yourself. There are several reasons for this. One, he may not always be in the organization; two, he may not always be around you; and, three, one should be so trained that he can function anywhere he is put—under any leadership or on his own.

Here are some of the problems you may encounter if you recruit a person to *yourself:*

a. Beware of pride. You are tempted to talk about *my* disciple, *my* team.

b. Beware of building emotionally dependent cripples. In building disciples we should be working ourselves spiritually out of a job, just as parents do in raising children. One of the objectives in child-rearing is to get your children to the point where they are independent of you, where they can go out on their own and make it in life. The same is true in the disciplemaking ministry. Disciples should increasingly grow more independent so they can go out on their own and work effectively for Christ.

c. Beware of making such a person unable to work with another leader. I have a couple of personal examples here. First, a negative one. We've had several people come from other disciplemaking ministries in America to our city. They were to work with me, as their team leader, in making disciples. But they didn't work out. It may have been that they were so identified with the personality of the person they had come from that they couldn't identify with my personality. On the other hand, it may have been my fault in giving poor leadership. But this happens far too often.

The other experience is positive and should be our objective in training disciples. I received a telephone call one day. The young man on the line gave me his name and said, "I am a graduate of the United States Air Force Academy. I was in a disciplemaking ministry there. I am now attending the medical school at the University of Oklahoma, and I want to meet you."

I said, "Fine, when can we get together?"

"What are you doing right now?" he queried.

"I am just sitting here at home," I replied.

He asked, "May I come by right now, sir?"

I answered, "You bet." In fifteen minutes he was in my home.

He announced, "I'm ready to go." No arguments, no questions. He was just ready to work for the Lord. He wasn't emotionally/spiritually crippled to the point where he could only work for his original leader. He had been trained to be a disciple for Christ . . . not a disciple for the one who made him a disciple.

In time there was a Bible study functioning every week in every class of the Medical Center. He is now a medical doctor on an Air Force Base with an effective on-going discipling ministry.

Some years ago, God gave me the privilege of working closely with a man from another nation and another culture. He was a foreign student with a brilliant mind, a striking personality, a tremendous knowledge of the Bible, and a love for God and people. Because of these qualities and attributes, nearly everywhere he went, he was adored, admired, and praised by people. Being interested in the fullest development of his character, I suggested that he work in one of our lumber yards one summer, and live with one of the men whom I had been discipling on a personal basis. In his country, the people who are educated do no manual labor. That is left for the uneducated. I knew that this would be a difficult decision for him. Also, moving in with someone who was leading a hard-nosed, disciplined life would not be the easiest assignment in the world. But he agreed.

The first week at the lumber yard, he was afraid he was going to die. The second week, he was afraid he wasn't. And about the fourth week, he said he'd like to get some time with me. So we made an appointment for one Sunday afternoon. The gist of what he said was that he felt God's will for him was to go to another city to take a job for the rest of the summer. I asked him which city he had in mind, and the two he named were cities where he happened to have friends who would put him up, take care of him, and not let him turn his hand.

I finally told him, "Friend, the door is open. You're free to go. But if you do, you will go against the counsel and the advice of those who love you. I believe that if you turn back at this point, you'll just be another ordinary itinerant preacher in your country instead of fulfilling all that I believe God has in mind for you." He left the home, and the next several days were excruciating and agonizing days of prayer. Finally, on Wednesday, I had a call from him. He said, "Sir, I've been praying, and I believe God would have me to stay." He did stay, and it was a real turning point in his life. But the door must always be left open for the learner to leave.

You're probably wondering at this point, If I'm to help others what will it cost me? Plenty, as you'll find out in the next chapter.

d. Beware lest they look to you instead of to God. This is the antithesis of what we want to produce. We want disciples who are sold out to Christ and to the concept of making other disciples.

Be sure the person understands that in being available to get help for his/her personal spiritual life, he/she isn't doing you or God a favor.

What is happening is that the disciple is receiving intimate personal help—the kind of help which few people in the world will ever have the opportunity to receive. One of the saddest verses in the Bible is Psalm 142:4, "I looked on my right hand, and beheld, but there was no man that would know me: refuge failed me; no man cared for my soul."

So, if God in His goodness and graciousness has given you the privilege of having someone who cares for your soul, you ought to thank God for that every day. The world is filled with people who do not have this privilege.

Help includes the whole person. There are no hidden areas; nothing is "off-limits." The disciple must be willing to open the life completely to you, as you must also do with the disciple.

The door must always be left open so the person can leave at any time. When the rich young ruler wouldn't heed Jesus' advice in Mark 10:17–22, Jesus allowed the door to be open for him to leave. The sad thing is that the young man did leave. Maybe some of your followers will leave. But that is best for them if they can't accept the loving counsel you give them.

5
How to Make Disciples

Part II: Helping People

So much in helping a young disciple grow is based on unseen spiritual laws, aspects of living where God works in the person's life. But delicate, loving guidance by the more experienced disciplemaker is imperative . . . to lead the disciple into the proper relationship with God so that the person will be receptive to God's Holy Spirit.

Every believer should receive help

1. *It is God's objective.* God wants us to become more and more like Jesus Christ day by day. "For whom he did foreknow, he also did predestinate to be conformed to the image of his Son, that he might be the firstborn among many brethren" (Rom 8:29). Paul goes on to say, "Till we all come in the unity of the faith, and of the knowledge of the Son of God, unto a perfect man, unto the measure of the stature of the fulness of Christ" (Eph. 4:13).

2. *Growth is commanded.* Peter says, "But grow in grace, and in the knowledge of our Lord and Savior Jesus Christ" (2 Peter 3:18).

3. *Growth is promised.* Paul assures us, "Being confident of this very thing, that he which hath begun a good work in you will perform it until the day of Jesus Christ" (Phil. 1:6).

4. *Growth is recommended.* Peter asks us:

Do you want more and more of God's kindness and peace? Then learn to know him better and better. For as you know him better, he will give you, through his great power, everything you need for living a truly good life: he even shares his own glory and his own goodness with us! And by that same mighty power he has given us all the other rich and wonderful blessings he promised; for instance, the promise to save us from the lust and rottenness all around us, and to give us his own character. But to obtain these gifts, you need more than faith; you must also work hard to be good, and even that is not enough. For then you must learn to know God better and discover what he wants you to do. Next, learn to put aside your own desires so that you will become patient and godly, gladly letting God have his way with you. This will make possible the next step, which is for you to enjoy other people and to like them, and finally you will grow to love them deeply. The more you go on in this way, the more you will grow strong spiritually and become fruitful and useful to our Lord Jesus Christ. But anyone who fails to go after these additions to faith is blind indeed, or at least very shortsighted, and has forgotten that God delivered him from the old life of sin so that now he can live a strong, good life for the Lord (2 Peter 1:2–9 LB).

5. *Growth is a lifelong process.* "Beloved, now are we the sons of God, and it doth not yet appear what we shall be: but we know that, when he shall appear, we shall be like him; for we shall see him as he is" (1 John 3:2). Until we see Him and become like Him, we are still a part of God's training program. The Institute of Basic Youth Conflicts gives buttons with these initials: PBPGIFWMY. This means "Please be patient. God isn't finished with me yet."

6. *When we refuse to grow, it is to our own hurt.* Luke tells us, " . . . but the Pharisees and the lawyers rejected the purpose of God for themselves, not having been baptized by him" (Luke 7:30 RSV). The only one who could thwart God's purpose for growth in our lives is ourselves. If we are following His will, no person, no group, no government can prevent His will being done in our lives.

God uses many means of growth

1. *His Word.* "Thy word is a lamp unto my feet, and a light unto my path" (Ps. 119:105).

2. *One's conscience.*
3. *The Holy Spirit.*
4. *Circumstances.*
5. *Other people.*

To be used of God to make disciples, we must be willing to pay the price . . . and it is a costly ministry.

1. *Costly in time.* We must be constantly on call. Moses prayed, "So teach us to number our days, that we may apply our hearts unto wisdom" (Ps. 90:12). Our time will not be our own. We must be available to those whom God has called us to help.

2. *Costly in lack of recognition.* Paul says, "Yet we urge you to have more and more of this love, and to make it your ambition to have no ambition! Be busy with your own affairs and do your work yourselves. The result will be a reputation for honesty in the world outside and an honourable independence" (1 Thess. 4:11,12 Phillips). The discipling ministry is not the kind that gets notoriety in the church paper. Neither is there a place to check it on your offering envelope. It is usually an unrecognized work in the kingdom of God. Other people may well get the notoriety while you continue to pour your life into others.

3. *Costly in inconvenience.* We are servants to those we intend to help. Jesus said, " . . . but I am among you as he that serveth" (Luke 22:27). We must meet the needs of those God has chosen for us to help. We meet those needs on God's terms, not on ours. We are, in fact, servants to the Body of Christ.

4. *Costly in hurt.* On this subject Paul wrote, "And I will very gladly spend and be spent for you; though the more abundantly I love you, the less I be loved" (2 Cor. 12:15). And in the same letter he added, "I pray that you will live good lives, not because that will be a feather in our caps, proving that what we teach is right; no, for we want you to do right even if we ourselves are despised" (2 Cor. 13:7 LB). He went on, "We are glad to be weak and

despised if you are really strong. Our greatest wish and prayer is that you will become mature Christians" (2 Cor. 13:9 LB). Some in whom you have invested your life will turn their backs on you and walk away. Others may even become bitter toward you. Still others will go so far in the school of discipleship and no further. All of these will hurt. We must not become discouraged in our calling, for some of those who fall by the wayside will eventually come back and want to get back on the path. Others are certainly better off for the help they have received than if they had received none at all.

5. *Costly in vulnerability to exposure.* Paul wrote to Timothy: "But thou hast fully known my doctrine, manner of life, purpose, faith, longsuffering, charity, patience, persecutions, afflictions, which came unto me at Antioch, at Iconium, at Lystra; what persecutions I endured: but out of them all the Lord delivered me" (2 Tim. 3:10,11). In the Phillips translation, this same verse reads: "But you, Timothy, have known intimately both what I have taught and how I have lived. My purpose and my faith are not secrets to you. You saw my endurance and love and patience as I met all those persecutions and difficulties. . . ."

You can't hide from the one you are helping! The one you are helping will see your feet of clay. A disciple will know your weaknesses because on an eyeball-to-eyeball basis, there is no place to hide.

6. *Costly in that you will be tunnelling while others are climbing.* Jeremiah said to Baruch, "And seekest thou great things for thyself? seek them not . . . " (Jer. 45:5). You will have to tunnel while others climb. But tunnelling is usually not very dangerous. When you climb sometimes rocks are kicked off and hit the people coming behind, but in tunnelling usually anyone can safely follow. Discipling people is a tunnelling ministry.

7. *Costly in seeing your weaknesses reproduced.* As it is in nature, so is it true in the Spirit . . . we reproduce in kind.

This is why "cross training" is so important. In cross training the disciple gets spiritual help from others beside yourself, so that all of your weaknesses aren't reproduced in that one. What Samuel learned as a little boy in Eli's family (bad habits of child-rearing), he reproduced in his own children. Then, at the end of Samuel's life the people saw the grave weaknesses in his children and asked that his children not be the rulers over them. A king had to be chosen from elsewhere. We do reproduce in kind.

8. *Costly in your life.* This is the main price we pay if we are going to disciple people. God said through Isaiah to his people Israel: "Since thou wast precious in my sight, thou hast been honourable, and I have loved thee: therefore will I give men for thee, and people for thy life" (43:4). That is exactly what it will cost you—your life.

6

How to Make Disciples

Part III: Motivation

One of the greatest single needs in Christendom today for fulfilling the Great Commission is the motivation of people. Unless people are motivated to evangelism, unless they are motivated to become disciples, unless they are motivated to make disciples, there is not going to be a great deal accomplished. Jesus said, "The harvest is plenteous, and the laborers are few." Why are the laborers not out in the harvest field? You ask a person why he/she did this or why he/she didn't do it, and inevitably the excuse comes back, "Because of this, or that, or the other thing." We need to motivate people by getting to the root of the "because." If one has the "want-to," we all have some idea of what to do with that person, to move him/her from being a convert to a disciple, and perhaps even a disciplemaker. But if one doesn't have the "want-to," if we cannot overcome the initial inertia, then what can be done? So we see that motivation is tremendously important.

They tell a story of a man who was walking through the graveyard late one night, after a big rain. Inadvertently he stumbled into an open grave. He tried as best he could to get out. He jumped up, he tried to climb, he tried to dig little footholes, but it seemed there was just no way out. So he decided he would wait until morning. Perhaps someone would come by and he could get help. Having made the decision, he sat quietly in one end of the grave. It wasn't long until another man came along and also stumbled into the grave. He tried diligently to get out but the more he tried it seemed the less able he was to climb the slippery wall. Then he heard a voice from the other end of the grave saying, "You can't get out of here." But he did!

That is motivation! In the Christian life, the I.Q. is not nearly as important as the M.Q. I.Q. stands for intelligence quotient. M.Q. stands for Motivational Quotient.

1. *What is motivation?* Someone has said motivation is to provide with a motive or a reason to impel, incite, invoke, or inspire. Another has said it's overcoming initial inertia. Someone else has said it's the inciting of an individual to action based on an internal force. Another has said it's the process of replacing individual goals with group objectives. Jesus said in Luke 9:24. "Whosoever shall save his life shall lose it, and whosoever shall lose his life for my sake, the same shall save it." My own working definition is: "Motivation is that force, either external or internal, which stimulates the spirit, soul, or body to respond."

2. *What motivates people?* There are four basic factors, two of which are rooted in selfishness. The things which should motivate us generally don't. Not many are motivated by the love that Christ has for them, by His death on the cross, by their love for Christ, their concern for a world of lost people on the way to hell, or for any of these good things which should motivate us. But people are motivated by:

a. *Conviction*—what a person really believes . . . deep within him. Peter had conviction. In Acts 5:29 (RSV) he said, "We must obey God." Paul had conviction. In Acts 20:24 (LB) he said, "But life is worth nothing unless I use it for doing the work assigned me by the Lord Jesus—the work of telling others the Good News about God's mighty kindness and love."

b. *Needs*. Needs come in three different forms. One, a person's *real needs*. The communists use this as a training tool. They will send a person to a certain place to preach the communist doctrine, where they know that one will fail. The person comes back in abject despair. *Then* he/she is motivated to have the proper training. He/she recognizes the need. In Acts 12 there was a real need. James had been killed by Herod. Because this murder pleased the Jews, Herod planned to kill Peter next. Peter was in prison. There was a real need for prayer. The church was motivated to pray, and Peter was delivered.

Two, a person's *felt needs*. This is when one feels he/she needs something but really doesn't. The eighth chapter of Acts tells us of Phillip going down to Samaria. There was a man by the name of Simeon who was a magician and a sorcerer. Simeon heard the gospel and was converted. Peter and John came down and Simeon saw that the laying on of their hands brought the Holy Spirit. So he offered them money in order that whoever he laid his hands on might receive the Holy Ghost. Peter told him, "Your money perish with you, because you thought the gift of God could be purchased with money." This was a felt need the sorcerer had. He wanted a shortcut. He wanted sudden spiritual maturity and power. It was a felt need, but the motivation was not Christian.

Three, one's *unconscious needs*. Once a young man came to me for discipleship training. He said, "I need help . . . I need training." But he didn't have anything specific in mind. I knew that this man had not missed a quiet time in years. He had memorized over two thousand verses. Yet he felt he needed more training. He had been in another city for three years and had produced no fruit in his ministry. He had an unconscious need. It took some time, but finally we discovered it. It was an emotional roadblock which was keeping this tremendously well-equipped man from being used of God. His self-image was so low that he could not believe that God could use him. Once it was discovered and removed, it became a new day for him. He is now having a splendid ministry.

In Mark 2 we find the story of the four men who brought a paralyzed friend on a bed and tore the roof off of the house to get him in front of Jesus. Jesus said, "Son, thy sins be forgiven thee." The man wasn't really interested in that. He didn't realize forgiveness was his need. He just wanted to be healed. Jesus knew that the removing of that block was necessary before his physical wholeness could come. And so it is that some people have unconscious needs. They reveal to you the surface problems, but unfortunately sometimes we just give them surface counsel. What we need to do, by the grace of God, is to look for the root problem and give them the counsel they need to strike at the heart of the difficulty. Then their unconscious need can be met.

c. *Goals.* Goals fall into three categories. Life goals, intermediate goals, and short-range goals. From the apostle Paul, we can get a look at the first two. His life goal is pointed out to us in Philippians: "For my determined purpose is that I may know Him, that I may progressively become more deeply and intimately acquainted with Him, perceiving and recognizing and understanding the wonders of His person more strongly and more clearly and that I may in that same way come to know the power outflowing from His resurrection which it exerts over believers and that I may so share His suffering as to be continually transformed in spirit into His likeness, even to His death" (3:10 Amplified). Paul's life goal was to know Jesus in an intimate way. His intermediate goal is revealed for us in Colossians 1:28,29: "So naturally we proclaim Christ. We warn everyone we meet and teach everyone we can all that we know about him so that if possible, we may present every man mature in Christ Jesus. That's what I'm working at all the time with all the strength that God gives me" (Phillips).

d. *Perspective.* How a person sees things determines

the extent and direction of their motivation. This is the reason Paul, in writing to the church in Colossae, said: "We are asking God that you may see things, as it were, from his point of view by being given spiritual insight and understanding. We also pray that your outward lives which men see may bring credit to your master's name and that you may bring joy to his heart by bearing genuine Christian fruit and that your knowledge of God may grow yet deeper" (Col. 1:9,10 Phillips).

When people begin to see things from God's point of view, they will be properly motivated to operate as God wishes them to operate.

| What do we need to motivate others? |

First, a motivating mind set. We need to think about it and get ready to do it.

Second, the right motive. We motivate others not for personal glory, or for personal power, but for the person's highest good and God's glory.

Third, the right attitude.

(1) Recognizing that the individual is of infinite worth. This worth is apparent in the cross of Christ.

(2) Believing in the limitless potential of each individual. Philippians 4:13 indicates that we can do all things through Christ which strengtheneth us. If we accept the basic fact that there is no limit to a person's capability, then we must also accept the fact that the need for motivation is always present in one's life in order that one might press on to all that God has planned.

Always love the person. Remember that Jesus said, "Having loved his own which were in the world, he loved them unto the end" (John 13:1). Love produces action and loyalty.

Never give up on the disciple. Jesus didn't give up on His followers. What if He had given up on Peter after he denied Him three times? He did not reject Judas even when he was bringing the soldiers. Did you ever notice what Jesus said in Matthew 26:50? *"Friend,* wherefore art thou come?" At that point, He still called Judas a friend. If we believe that God can make any person a significant individual, we will not give up on others. Actually, we receive from people pretty well what we expect of them. I guess we can give up on another person when Christ gives up on us. The teaching is clear in the New Testament. The essential meaning of forgiveness is not simply to pardon, but to heal. Many times Christ said, "Be made whole." And often the wholeness of a person is dependent on our not giving up. It is dependent on our forgiving and believing in that one. Jesus believes in me. He keeps on forgiving and believing in me until one day, by His grace and power, He will transform me totally into His likeness. That's the teaching of Philippians 1:6: "Being confident of this very thing, he which hath begun a good work in you will perform it until the day of Jesus Christ." Always love a disciple and never give up on him.

Get involved

(1) Discover the person's convictions, needs, goals, and perspective: what one really believes; what one's real wants are; where one wants to go; how one sees things.

This is not easy. We must listen, probe, retreat, pray, listen, probe, retreat, pray, listen, probe, retreat, and pray. And then repeat the above.

We must strengthen our personal relationship with the disciple to help build convictions. To do this we must have some convictions of our own. There are some ways we can help others. We can have them do a study on whatever we'd like for them to build a conviction about—perhaps on the servant heart or the multiplication principle, or even the principle of one-on-one. Or ask the person to do a workshop in a conference. Or to bring a message in a conference on the subject. Suggest some tapes for the person to listen to, or some books to read. We build convictions by helping a person develop his/her thinking. It is not simply by the force of logic. We change people's thinking by humility, empathy, understanding, and involvement.

(2) Meet the person's needs. Admittedly, most people's needs will be selfish. But whether they are selfish or not, if you are to motivate people, those needs must be met.

(3) Remove emotional roadblocks. In the first six verses of John 5 we have the story of the man who had been crippled for thirty-eight years and continued to stay by the sheep market at a pool called Bethesda. The people believed that when an angel stirred the water, the first one to get in the water would be healed. Seeing the man, Jesus asked him if he wanted to be healed. That seems a strange question to ask a man who has been crippled for thirty-eight years and who was trying desperately to get into the water on time. But the facts are that some people don't want to be healed. They would rather "enjoy ill health" than be made whole. The question was whether or not the man had an emotional roadblock keeping him from having his need met.

(4) *Help people set worthy goals.* They must be personal goals, but we can always help.

(5) *Have a game plan.* Always love the person and never give up on him/her.

Set clear standards. Make it clear where one is supposed to be heading and the route one is expected to take. Let the person know how he/she is progressing. Communicate it clearly. To really communicate, the message must be received, it must be understood, and it must be accepted.

Let the disciple know you care if he/she sinks or swims. In 1 Corinthians 13:8 Paul says love never fails.

Express confidence in the person and demonstrate it. In Acts 20:32 when Paul was with the elders at Ephesus and had told them that they would not see Him again, He then made this interesting statement: "And now, brethren, I commend you to God and to the word of his grace which is able to build you up and to give you an inheritance among all them which are sanctified." He demonstrated tremendous confidence in them by commending them to God and to His Word.

Let the person learn by mistakes. Remember the story of Jesus coming to the men during the storm walking on the water. They were afraid. He said, "Don't be afraid, it's me." And Peter said, "Lord, if it's You, then bid me come to You." And Jesus said, "Come." Well, Peter stepped out of the boat and began to walk on the water. Then he looked at the waves and the wind and began to sink. He then prayed one of the most effective prayers ever prayed. It may not have been a highly theological prayer but it certainly was effective. He simply prayed, "Lord, save me!" And of course, Jesus did (see Matt. 14:23–31). Hopefully, Peter learned from that mistake that we need to keep our eyes on Jesus, not on the seeming problems.

Create needs in the person. Get the person in over his/her head. And then the person will know that more training is needed. Stretch the disciple. Remember in the fourth chapter of Mark, Jesus gave a tremendous lecture on the kingdom of God, faith, the Word, a grain of mustard seed, and so on. Then He said to His followers, "Let's cross the lake." So they got out on the lake and a storm came up. Jesus was asleep. The disciples thought the waves were going to swamp the boat. They came back to Him and asked, "Don't you care if we drown? Help us!" Then He calmed the storm and said, "Where is your faith?" The lesson He was teaching is this. "Remember, men. I gave you that tremendous lecture on faith, and now here's a demonstration. I didn't say, 'Let's go to the lake and get drowned.' I said, 'Let's go across the lake.' "

Jesus demonstrated this again in John 4 when He got into the conversation with the woman at the well. He finally said to her, "There's another kind of water. The kind that springs up into everlasting life." She said, "I didn't know that. Let me have some of it." He created a need within her.

We have the privilege of creating needs within those with whom we work. We might say to someone some day, "Listen, you can be a part of the movement that is changing the world. And I believe God's going to use you in a significant way in the lives of many in the days to come." It might be the turning point for that person for all eternity. That's known as visualizing success for your people.

A man once came to be with me for help in training and told me when he arrived that he would do anything I wanted him to do. He'd wash my car, cut my grass, shine my shoes, run errands, anything I wanted, except he simply could not speak in front of people. Well, you know the first thing I did was to get him up in front of people, and it scared him to death. But it wasn't long, as I watched him, until I recognized what I thought to be the gift of teaching in him. One day I told him, "Friend, I believe that God has given you the gift of teaching. And I believe that the time will come when you'll be teaching the Word of God not only in Oklahoma City and around this nation, but around the world." He could not have looked more surprised. But God in His graciousness has brought it to pass. I had visualized that for him, he came to the place by faith believing that God could use him, and just recently he had the privilege of traveling for nearly two months around the world, preaching the unsearchable riches of Christ from the Word of God.

Equip the person to do the job. In the first chapter of Jeremiah and in Exodus 4 we see two examples of God's special equipping of people. In Jeremiah, God wanted to send him to be a prophet of the people. Jeremiah said, "I can't speak—I'm a child." God said, "Wait a minute. I'll be your mouth. Don't be afraid." He equipped him to do the job. And when Moses was afraid to accept the job of leading the children of Israel out of Egypt, God gave him the sign of the rod and the serpent, and also the sign of the leprous hand being cleansed and said, "Now I've equipped you. Go do it." *We*, too, can help equip a person through the example of our lives, and through personally teaching and training him in the Word.

Be fair, impartial, and consistent. Psalm 106:3 (LB) "Happiness comes to those who are fair to others and are always just and good." Give the credit to your disciples, always share the blame.

Let the disciple help decide, where possible, what he or she is going to do, and the way to do it. Paul says in Romans 14:12, "So then every one of us shall give an account of himself to God." We need to make the disciple as independent of us as we can.

Check-up. Someone said that the best fertilizer for any job is the footprints of the boss. People may not do what we *expect* but they are usually more likely to do what we *inspect:* "Riches can disappear fast, and the king's crown doesn't stay in his family forever, so watch your business interest closely. Know the state of your flocks and your herds" (Prov. 27:23,24 LB). This certainly has a spiritual application. Know how your people are getting along.

Show encouragement and appreciation: "Anxious hearts are very heavy, but a word of encouragement does wonders" (Prov. 12:25 LB). Know what to get enthusiastic about. Reinforce the disciple by commendation. Be enthused with and about the person. Be encouraging. Someone said, "If you want him to bleed, hemorrhage!"

Empathize with the disciple and pay the price. "I'm not saying this to scold or blame you, for as I have said before, you are in my heart forever and I live and die with you" (2 Cor. 7:3 LB). "As Christ's cup of suffering overflows and we suffer with him, so also through Christ our consolation overflows" (2 Cor 1:5 NEB). To motivate effectively, we must understand people and have the will power to force ourselves to do what we have determined should be done. This boils down to empathy and determination. One who has a high degree of empathy, that is, the ability to get with a person, and is able to subordinate his/her personal ideas and preferences to the objective being sought, can be an effective motivator. Empathy means putting yourself in the other's place. When you do that, you're not likely to bail out. In Matthew 26:40 Jesus asked His men, "Could ye not watch with me one hour?" Paul said, "Demas hath forsaken me, having loved this present world" (2 Tim. 4:10). But in 1 Peter 4:13 Peter indicates that we ought to rejoice because we are partakers of Christ's suffering. We are empathizing with the disciple. Don't bail out. Always love people and never give up on them.

Be a consistent example. In 1 Corinthians 11:1 Paul said, "Be ye followers of me, even as I also am of Christ." In Philippians 4:9 he said, "Those things, which ye have both learned, and received, and heard, and seen in me, do. And the God of peace shall be with you." Follow the Master closely. Invite others to follow you. I believe that every person alive wants to do the best job possible.

| Hindrances to motivation |

(1) Lack of concern. "Let nothing be done through strife or vainglory, but in lowliness of mind, let each esteem other better than themselves. Look not every man on his own things, but every man also on the things of others" (Phil. 2:3,4).

(2) Lack of personal contact. In Acts 15:36 we are told: "And some days after Paul said unto Barnabas, Let us go again and visit our brethren in every city where we have preached the word of the Lord, and see how they do." That is keeping in touch.

(3) A lack of listening. "He that answereth a matter before he heareth it, it is folly and shame unto him" (Prov. 18:13). "Wherefore, my beloved brethren, let every man be swift to hear, slow to speak, slow to wrath" (James 1:19).

(4) A lack of thinking and planning. "The testimony of a liar is not believed, but the word of someone who thinks things through is accepted" (Prov. 21:28 GNB). "For want of skillful strategy an army is lost. Victory is the fruit of long planning" (Prov. 11:14 NEB). "We should make plans—counting on God to direct us" (Prov. 16:9 LB).

(5) A lack of prayer. In 1 Thessalonians 5:25 Paul says, "Brethren, pray for us." In 2 Thessalonians 3:1 he says, "Finally, brethren, pray for us that the word of the Lord may have free course, and be glorified, even as it is with you." In Romans 15:30 (LB), he says, "Will you be my prayer partners? For the Lord Jesus Christ's sake, and because of your love for me—given to you by the Holy Spirit—pray much with me for my work." We will never motivate others until we pray for them, for their goals, their objectives, their needs.

Measuring motivation

You can measure how well you are doing in terms of the person's progress. Over a period of time there should be improvement, even though there will be ups and downs in terms of specific progress. If it is a team you are motivating, you can measure it in terms of the individual team member's progress and the effectiveness of the team.

Remember that it is a never-ending process

It is a lifetime job. The needs are never completely met. The problems are never completely solved. The emotional roadblocks are never completely removed. No one arrives in this life, and therefore it is a process of trial and error—and prayer.

Do not be discouraged

If the goal that we have for the people we are trying to motivate is God's goal for them, then we do not work alone.

(1) The Bible is building conviction in their lives.

(2) The Bible is giving them God's perspective.

(3) Jesus is meeting their needs (Phil. 4:19).

(4) Our goal and our marching orders are clear—the Great Commission. God wants us to become more and more like Jesus day by day.

(5) God is working with our friend also.

(a) Through circumstances. "And we know that all things work together for good for them that love God, to them who are the called according to his purpose" (Rom. 8:28). Therefore, as Paul says in 1 Thessalonians 5:18, "In every thing give thanks."

(b) By the Holy Spirit. "And thine ear shall hear a word behind thee saying, This is the way, walk ye in it, when ye turn to the right hand, and when ye turn to the left" (Isa. 30:21).

(c) Through other believers. "As iron sharpeneth iron; so a man sharpeneth the countenance of his friend" (Prov. 27:17).

(6) Motivation is always a two-way street. We never help others but that we ourselves get help. Earlier in the book I shared how I came to know the Lord and how two men on the Billy Graham team had meant so much to my own life from the standpoint of helping my own relationship to be very personal with Christ. I wish I could report that from that point on everything was peaches and cream, but it wasn't.

Three years after the crusade I was with my wife and three daughters at our lake cabin waterskiing. We'd had a great time and my wife had almost insisted that I attend a conference for men at a Christian conference grounds in Colorado. So I left on Sunday, picked up three other fellows, and drove toward the conference grounds. On Monday noon my wife came back to town and between Monday noon and Tuesday afternoon, bought and charged $6,200 worth of clothes to me. Then she filed suit for divorce.

It came as a complete shock and surprise to me. We had been married fifteen years. Her bill of particulars accused me of terrible moral impurity. No divorce is ever a one-way street; it still takes two to tango. I certainly do not put the fault of the divorce totally at her feet, and I'm sure that I made most of the mistakes that a husband can make. However, it just happened that the things of which I was accused in the moral realm were not true. Our story received good front page coverage in the city where I had been raised and where I was attempting to make a living. I was accused on the front page of being everything a man ought not to be. I considered suicide. I considered murder. I even considered getting together what money I could and leaving the country. I found out what countries you could go to from which the courts couldn't get you back. They were Portugal and Spain. At that time, they did not have tradition treaties with our country. I considered going back to the bottle, or just living for pleasure alone. But then I had another thought. I decided that if Jesus Christ could not see me through this situation, He might not be able to take care of me down at the end of the road of life. So my decision was to sit still and see what happened.

The divorce fought through the courts for four and a half years. It was an excruciating time. I began to get some victory when I became more interested in what God knew than what people thought. And then I finally realized that there was no edict which the judge could hand down which could affect my relationship to Christ. If my relationship with Christ was still intact, and I was healthy of body and mind, by the grace of God, I'd make it. I thought, of course, that my ministry was over. I submitted my resignation to the Sunday school class I was teaching; I resigned as a member of the ruling body of the church. I told the couples I was leading in Bible study that I'd lead them no longer. The church refused to accept my resignation, either from Sunday school or the ruling body. The couples told me they were going to meet anyway, and I was welcome to join them. God, in His mercy and grace, allowed me to continue to minister. It looked like in the midst of the proceedings that I was going to be worse than bankrupt. You know, you can be worse than broke. Once you've looked that spectre in the face, it can't scare you again. Looking back on it from today, if God would give me the power to turn back the hands of time to the day the divorce was filed, and allow me to re-rig the circumstances any way that I'd like to change them, I would not touch them.

Many people know intellectually that Romans 8:28 is true, that all things do work together for good to those who love God. But I have the inexpressible privilege of knowing it experientially. Regardless of the pain and the cost in every way, it was worth it. I'm a slow learner and I learned some things about God in those days which I do not believe I would have learned any other way. And then if the divorce had not happened, I would have missed my precious wife Irma and our three wonderful sons. I do not believe that God broke up my first family. If He did, He will have to rewrite the Bible. I believe it was an attack of the enemy. However, it makes no difference what the source of the problem is, if our response is proper, God can use it for our good and His glory. The reason I share this part of my life at this point is to reveal to you the facts that motivation comes from many places, many directions, and has many faces. But in it all, God can be glorified, and God can use it if we are willing to let Him.

Your own life is the most important tool in motivation

Always love the person you're working with and never give up on him or her. One reason we ought not to give up is our knowledge of ourselves. In Proverbs 20:27, the writer says, "The Lord gave us mind and conscience; we cannot hide from ourselves" (GNB). In 1 Timothy 4:16 Paul says, "Keep a close watch on all you do and think.

Stay true to what is right and God will bless you and use you to help others" (LB).

> When you get what you want in your struggle for self,
> And the world makes you king for a day,
> Just go to a mirror and look at yourself,
> And see what the man has to say.
>
> It isn't your father or mother or wife,
> Whose judgment on you must pass,
> The fellow whose verdict counts most in your life
> Is the one staring back from the glass.
>
> You may be a Jack Horner and chisel a plum,
> And think you're a wonderful guy.
> But that man in the glass says you're only a bum
> If you can't look him straight in the eye.
>
> He's the fellow to please—never mind all the rest.
> For he's with you clear up to the end.
> And you've passed your most dangerous, difficult test
> If the man in the glass is your friend.
>
> *—Author Unknown*

Before going on, it might be well for you to take stock of yourself in the area of your own ability as a motivator. Be as honest and objective as you possibly can. Grade yourself on the following questions in accordance with this code.

5—Always; 90–100 percent of the time
4—Most of the time; 60–80 percent of the time
3—About half the time; 41–59 percent of the time
2—Sometimes; 11–40 percent
1—Seldom; 1–10 percent of the time
0—Never or practically never

__1. Do you make a conscious effort to get people to really want to do anything you ask them to do?

__2. Do you ascertain whether there is actual agreement

before using the plural, "we," in stating your ideas or opinions?

__3. In attempting to motivate other people, do you make a sincere effort to see things *their* way?

__4. In your relations with others, are you ready, willing, and able to be influenced (changed) by them?

__5. Are you sensitive to the *personal* factors which affect people's attitudes toward things?

__6. Are you able to imaginatively project yourself into other people—to really imagine yourself in their "shoes"?

__7. Are you successful in getting other people to revise their goals and objectives?

__8. Do you assist others in determining what they are really "after"—what they really want out of life?

__9. Do you find it easy to adapt yourself to different individuals and circumstances?

__10. Are you conscious of the fact that the "problem" of motivating can really never be "solved"?

__11. Do you think of motivation as something which must be continually *improved?*

__12. When you attempt to get people to do something, do you convince them that it is to their personal advantage to do it?

__13. When people disagree with you, do you try to discover the real reason for their disagreement?

__14. Do you attempt to explore other people's personal, perhaps even subconscious, reasons for thinking as they do?

__15. Do you influence other people without even letting them know that you are influencing them?

__16. Do you honestly feel that you can learn something from everyone and everything you come into contact with?

__17. Are you aware of the fact that motivation is a continually changing thing and that what worked yesterday may not work today?

__18. Do you exert a deliberate, conscious effort to avoid assuming that others think as you do?

__19. Are you fully aware of the fact that people often don't know themselves what they really want—and do you act accordingly?

__20. Do you have an established policy of considering long-range objectives in your dealings with people?

__21. When you are confronted with a difficulty, do you take time out to make sure that you have really defined the problem before taking action?

__22. Do you exert a sincere effort to avoid always taking the same approach to the same problem?

__23. Do you take account of the fact that people quite often say things which differ appreciably from what they *think?*

__24. Do you make a deliberate effort to avoid judging people by outward appearances or actions?

__25. When you discover that people are not being quite honest with themselves, do you attempt to bring this to their attention?

__26. Do you make a sincere effort to avoid discussions about what you have said when it has apparently been misunderstood?

__27. Do you make it a practice to explain team long-term and short-term plans and objectives to everyone concerned?

__28. Do you accept the fact that optimum performance simply cannot be achieved by means of fear, force, or coercion?

__29. Do you have confidence in the ability of other people to perform satisfactorily?

__30. Having started someone on some project, do you check periodically to determine whether that person is proceeding properly and according to schedule?

__31. Do you avoid cut-and-dried methods of motivation and make a real effort to help people to motivate themselves?

__32. Do you go out of your way to assure people that they are really important?

__33. Do you avoid "throwing your weight around," "pulling rank," or otherwise reminding people that they are dependent on you?

__34. Do you recognize that those you attempt to motivate probably think differently than you do?

__35. Do you go out of your way to assure people that they are an important part of the "team"?

__36. Do you take account of the fact that most people have a tendency to "kid themselves"?

__37. Do you make a point of commending people on outstanding performance at least as frequently as you call their attention to deficiencies in their performance?

__38. Do you go out of your way to take a positive approach to things—and to let people know that you do?

__39. Do you concentrate on fundamentals rather than on details?

__40. Do you go out of your way to encourage people?

__41. Are you willing to let other people take the credit for what you have accomplished?

__42. Do you recognize the fact that your team members, as well as the other team leaders and superiors, have to perform all the so-called "management" functions you perform?

__43. Do you provide those you deal with with clear-cut indications of just what you expect from them and how much individual latitude they may exercise?

__44. Do you make people convince you that their ideas are correct, and do you assure yourself that they have really convinced themselves?

__45. Do you deliberately restrain yourself from interfering when you see someone else about to make a mistake?

__46. Do you avoid hiding behind the "excuse" that you have the responsibility but not the authority you need?

__47. Do you ascertain that those you are trying to motivate know exactly what is expected of them?

___48. Do you make it a point to let those you motivate know whether they are progressing properly and on schedule—both when they are and when they are not?

___49. When you attempt to motivate people, do you make sure that they possess whatever it might take to accomplish what they are expected to accomplish?

___50. Do you make it perfectly clear to those you are trying to motivate, *why* they must do what you are requesting them to do?

___51. Do you try to make sure that competition is restricted to a friendly, cooperative effort to reach a common objective?

___52. Are you open to suggestions and constructive criticism from those you attempt to motivate?

___53. Do you give your immediate leader the advantage of your best thoughts and ideas without reservation?

___54. Do you make a conscious effort to treat yourself exactly the same way you treat everyone else?

___55. When you make suggestions, do you make absolutely sure that they have been heard (or read) properly?

___56. When you make suggestions, do you make absolutely sure that, not only the suggestion itself, but also the *reasons* for it, are thoroughly understood?

___57. When you make suggestions, do you make sure that the person receiving the suggestion realizes that it is beneficial to comply?

___58. Do you reprove, rebuke, or correct only as a last resort—and in private?

___59. Do you avoid demonstrating your personal knowledge or ability to your co-laborers?

___60. Do you demonstrate a real, personal interest in the suggestions of others?

___61. Do you make it a policy to evaluate any situation as best you can and then take a definite stand on it?

___62. Do you do everything in your power to keep your team members well-informed on policy, procedure, and plans for the future?

___63. Do you make a real effort to avoid becoming involved in unimportant details?

___64. Do you try to detect and eliminate friction between your team members?

___65. Do you go out of your way to let your team members know that you have confidence in their ability?

___66. Do you try to make your team members believe that they are just as important to the group effort as you are?

___67. Do you try to be courteous and considerate in your dealings with others?

___68. Are you alert to hidden meanings?

___69. Have you established a list of fundamentals which will assist you in motivating others, and do you review it periodically to update it?

___70. Do you honestly and sincerely trust the capacity of your team members for self-direction?

___71. Do you recognize the function of motivating people as one of your most important functions?

___72. Do you recognize which of your personal characteristics have the most important effect on your motivating ability?

___73. Do you make a deliberate, sincere effort to analyze your own motives when you encounter disagreement or resistance?

___74. Are you aware that people's needs change from day to day, and are you on the alert to detect such changes?

___75. Do you assure a free and uninhibited communications atmosphere before attempting to motivate?

___76. Do you approach the matter of motivating with full knowledge that it is a *mutual* undertaking requiring *mutual* understanding?

___77. Are you sensitive to other people's moods?

___78. Are you personally embarrassed when someone else makes a mistake?

___79. Do you fully recognize that anyone can do anything better if one really *wants* to?

__80. Do you (at least mentally) categorize people according to how much motivating they require to perform satisfactorily?

__81. Are you willing to accept things that you do not fully understand?

__82. Do you continually strive to improve your motivating ability?

__83. Do you fully accept the fact that you cannot obtain real cooperation by force?

__84. Do you make use of the fact that you can actually persuade people by *listening* to them?

__85. Do you fully understand the psychological aspects of motivating people?

__86. Do you avoid seeking recognition for your accomplishments?

__87. Do you recognize that you are undoubtedly learning more from your team members than they are learning from you?

__88. Do you make a real effort to remove (or relieve) motivating "pressures" when you feel they are no longer needed?

__89. Do you consciously avoid enforcing your standards on others?

__90. Are you pretty good at getting down to the real cause of the problem?

__91. Do you really grasp all pertinent factors and place each in its proper perspective in relation to the whole?

__92. Do you refuse to allow yourself to be annoyed by minor complaints?

__93. Do you make a deliberate attempt to find new approaches to problems?

__94. Do you make a sincere attempt to analyze your own motives—and to assist others to analyze theirs?

__95. Do you make a deliberate effort to avoid arguing with people who seem to be unusually argumentative?

__96. Do you try to lead others *to their own conclusions* rather than impress yours on them?

___97. Do you really try to explain to others how and why you arrived at your own conclusions?

___98. Do you go out of your way to make others understand what basic team objectives (rather than individual goals) really are?

___99. Have you exerted a real effort to master the discipling ministry as a discipline in its own right?

___100. Has your motivating ability (and methods) advanced along with the growth and maturity?

___101. Do you deliberately try to inspire people to work toward certain goals?

___102. Do you recognize that people in general really want to do the best possible job?

___103. Do you go out of your way to help others build an acceptable self-image?

___104. Do you really want to treat *everyone* else as an "equal"?

___105. Do you try, insofar as possible, to make others feel that they are the "masters of their own destinies"?

___106. Do you recognize that today's goals will not suffice for tomorrow?

___107. Do you make use of some systematic method for determining which of several factors is most important?

___108. Do you accept your position as a "supporting" one?

___109. Do you discipline your team members in private and reward them in public?

___110. Do you honestly believe that you are capable of motivating people effectively?

___111. Do you avoid telling other people about their limitations?

_____SCORE

ANALYSIS

SCORE	MOTIVATING EFFECTIVENESS
460–555	Excellent
400–459	Very good
360–399	Good
315–359	Fair
270–314	Poor
Less than 270	You need help, friend

7

How to Make Disciples

Part IV: Teaching and Training

By definition, teaching is imparting knowledge. Telling isn't teaching. Neither is listening learning. We know we have really taught when there is a heartfelt change in behavior. In a disciplemaking ministry we teach the disciple how to have an effective personal walk with Christ. As we pointed out in chapter 2, a disciple is a learner—which calls for someone to teach and train him. And what do we teach?

A personal walk with Christ:

1. *Quiet Time.* Have a daily personal time of spiritual nourishment alone with God. It is generally best to have this the first thing in the morning, so as to start the day with the Lord and so that it won't be relegated to a secondary "to do" item. David says, "My voice shalt thou hear in the morning, O Lord; in the morning will I direct my prayer unto thee, and will look up" (Ps. 5:3). Cliff Barrows gave me the Inter-Varsity Christian Fellowship booklet, *Quiet Time.* It came as a shock to me that the Creator of the universe desired fellowship with me. That is still a staggering thought. But one night, as the crusade was drawing near to its close in Oklahoma City, I was on the platform with Cliff Barrows putting away the lapel mike,

the pulpit, and so forth, when he hit me with the loaded question, "Gene, when do you have your quiet time?"

I asked, "What do you mean, Cliff?"

He asked again, "When do you read your Bible?" I told him that I read my Bible daily, but that didn't get the proper response. Then he asked me when I prayed. I told him I prayed before I went to bed at night and sometimes even prayed driving down the road. But since his ears didn't light up, I recognized that I had missed it there, too. He said, "I'll give you a little book, if you will read it."

"How long will it take?" I asked.

He said, "About forty-five minutes."

I promised, "I'll read it." And he gave me Inter-Varsity Christian Fellowship's *Quiet Time* booklet. I took it home that night and read it, and began the next morning meeting the Lord in a personal time of fellowship. It really revolutionized my life. I personally believe that the daily quiet time is the least common denominator of a vital, consistent, dynamic walk with Jesus, and I would give up every other discipline in the Christian life before I would give up that one.

2. *The necessity of the Word.* It appears to me that people have been used by God in direct proportion to how well they have been equipped with the Word of God. There are five ways to get the Word into one's life:

a. Hearing. "So then faith cometh by hearing, and hearing by the word of God" (Rom. 10:17).

b. Reading. "Blessed is he that readeth, and they that hear the words of this prophecy, and keep those things which are written therein: for the time is at hand" (Rev. 1:3).

c. Studying. "Study to shew thyself approved unto God, a workman that needeth not to be ashamed, rightly dividing the word of truth" (2 Tim. 2:15).

d. Memorizing. "Acquaint now thyself with him, and be at peace: thereby good shall come unto thee. Receive,

I pray thee, the law from his mouth, and lay up his words in thine heart" (Job 22:21,22).

e. Meditating. "This book of the law shall not depart out of thy mouth; but thou shalt meditate therein day and night, that thou mayest observe to do according to all that is written therein: for then thou shalt make thy way prosperous, and then thou shalt have good success" (Josh. 1:8).

I have given you the ways of taking in the Word of God in inverse order of their effectiveness. We only retain about 10–15 percent of what we hear. We retain something like 25 percent of what we read, 50–60 percent of what we study, all of what we memorize if we review it. Of course, meditation used with each one of the other means of taking in the Word of God—hearing, reading, studying, and memorizing—is a way that we get it from our head to our heart, and out into our life. Again, with this, it's not either/or, but both/and.

3. *Prayer.* You can remember the four basic types of prayer with the acronym ACTS: *A*doration, *C*onfession, *T*hanksgiving, and *S*upplication.

a. Adoration. "Whoso offereth praise glorifieth me: and to him that ordereth his conversation aright will I shew the salvation of God" (Ps. 50:23).

b. Confession. "If we confess our sins, he is faithful and just to forgive us our sins, and to cleanse us from all unrighteousness" (1 John 1:9).

c. Thanksgiving. "In every thing give thanks: for this is the will of God in Christ Jesus concerning you" (1 Thess. 5:18).

d. Supplication (1) for others: "Moreover as for me, God forbid that I should sin against the Lord in ceasing to pray for you . . ." (1 Sam. 12:23). Supplication (2) for yourself: "Be careful for nothing; but in every thing by prayer and supplication with thanksgiving let your requests be made known unto God. And the peace of God, which passeth all understanding, shall keep your hearts and minds through Christ Jesus" (Phil. 4:6,7).

Training techniques

Training can be defined simply as imparting skills. Webster's dictionary says to train is "to instruct or drill in habits of thought or action: shape or develop the character of by discipline or precept."

How does one train in disciplemaking? The primary way is by example. Someone once said that example is not *a* way of training, it is the *only* way. The following simple poem expresses the concept concisely:

I'd rather see a sermon than hear one any day.
I'd rather one should walk with me than merely show the way.
The eye's a better pupil and more willing than the ear;
Fine counsel is confusing, but example's always clear;
And the best of all the preachers are the men who live their creeds,
For to see the good in action is what everybody needs.
I can soon learn how to do it, if you'll let me see it done.
I can watch your hands in action, but your tongue too fast may run.
And the lectures you deliver may be very wise and true;
But I'd rather get my lesson by observing what you do.
For I may misunderstand you and the high advice you give,
But there's no misunderstanding how you act and how you live.

—*Edgar A. Guest*

His ministry

1. *Evangelism.* The young disciple must be helped in the fundamentals of how to evangelize. This begins as one learns how to give a testimony of one's personal encounter with Jesus Christ. Then the disciple should be given instruction in the use of certain tools which assist in the evangelism process: such items as the "Bridge Tract," published by the Navigators; "The Four Spiritual Laws,"

published by Campus Crusade for Christ International; *Steps to Peace with God*, by the Billy Graham Evangelistic Association. Finally, the disciple should be thoroughly taught the scripture verses on the gospel so that when he/she talks to another person about Christ (evangelizing) he/she can give biblical evidence.

2. *Fellowship.* The disciple needs to learn the value of operating as part of a team. There are eight aspects of this:

a. Learning to get along with others. "And Jesus increased in wisdom and stature, and in favour with God and man" (Luke 2:52). "And herein do I exercise myself, to have always a conscience void of offence toward God, and toward men" (Acts 24:16).

b. Fulfilling Jesus' prayer for unity. See John 17.

c. Gaining spiritual strength. "Two are better than one; because they have a good reward for their labor. For if they fall, the one will lift up his fellow: but woe to him that is alone when he falleth; for he hath not another to help him up. . . . And if one prevail against him, two shall withstand him; and a threefold cord is not quickly broken" (Eccl. 4:9,10,12). Willingness to depend on others is an important spiritual lesson.

d. Increasing power in ministry. "Five of you will chase a hundred, and a hundred of you, ten thousand! You will defeat all of your enemies" (Lev. 26:8 LB). I'm not too good at mathematics, but it looks like the increased numbers make the people about five times more effective. I like the way God figures this in His economy.

e. Increasing power in prayer. "Again, I say unto you, That if two of you shall agree on earth as touching anything that they shall ask, it shall be done for them of my Father which is in heaven. For where two or three are gathered together in my name, there am I in the midst of them" (Matt. 18:19,20). For some reason, which I do not understand, your faith plus my faith when we are apart, is not nearly as strong as the sum total of our faiths when we are together. It may be that my faith is strengthened by yours and yours by mine. It may be a case of us propping each other up on the leaning side. But whatever the case may be, the prayer of people joining together is more effective than the sum totals of their prayer when they are apart.

f. Protection. "Iron sharpeneth iron; so a man sharpeneth the countenance of his friend" (Prov. 27:17). "But exhort one another daily, while it is called today; lest any of you be hardened through the deceitfulness of sin" (Heb. 3:13).

g. Peer group pressure. I find myself so lazy and slothful that if I'm not doing Bible study with a group, I simply won't do Bible study. But if I know that I'm going to meet with ten people at six o'clock on Saturday morning, and they're going to have their Bible study assignments prepared, then I intend by the grace of God to have mine prepared. This used to make me feel guilty until I began to realize that God knows our frame, that we are dust, and that He has provided this peer group pressure as a way to help us function as we should.

h. It works. Look at the teamwork and cooperation in such agencies as the Mayo Clinic and NASA, with its spectacular space shots. Neither the Mayo Clinic or NASA could have accomplished what they have accomplished apart from teamwork.

3. *Follow-up.* This is spiritual pediatrics. It covers what to do with a new babe in Christ, how to do it, and when.

4. *How to lead a group Bible study.*

5. *How to speak to groups.*

6. *Basic Bible doctrine.*

7. *Bible prophecy.*

8. *Principles of spiritual multiplication.*

9. *The infinite potential and worth of the individual.*

Here are some things to do with your disciple:

1. Have a quiet time together for awhile.

2. Get the disciple into a Bible study with you to show him/her how to study properly and apply the Bible to everyday living.

3. Check Scripture memory verses together; and let your disciple review you on yours.

4. Have prayer together.

5. Evangelize together. You witness, give your testimony, and explain the gospel. Little by little let the disciple do the same, until he/she can do it all alone. (See the story of Ted in Chapter 1).

6. Expose the disciple to other Christians. Cross training is invaluable.

7. Give responsibility. Trust God and trust the learner. Allow the disciple to make mistakes.

8. Give structured learning opportunities with books, tapes, films, and resource people.

Possible problems in training disciples

A. Zeal can get out of balance. We can become so zealous in one approach or one method that the whole thing is thrown out of balance. *We are out of balance and off center when any of the following occur:*

1. When in our determination to be bold, we become brazen.

> And Paul, earnestly beholding the council, said, Men and brethren, I have lived in all good conscience before God until this day. And the high priest Ananias commanded them that stood by him to smite him on the mouth. Then said Paul unto him, God shall smite thee, thou whited wall: for sittest thou to judge me after the law, and commandest me to be smitten contrary to the law? And they that stood by said, Revilest thou God's high priest? Then said Paul, I wist not, brethren, that he was the high priest: for it is written, Thou shalt not speak evil of the ruler of thy people (Acts 23:1–5).

This was an example where Paul's boldness, a strength, got out of hand and became insensitive brazenness.

2. When, in our desire to become frank, we become rude. "Love is not arrogant or rude" (1 Cor. 13:5). "Most important of all, continue to show deep love for one another, for love makes up for many of your faults" (1 Peter 4:8 LB).

3. When, in our effort to be watchful, we become suspicious. "An evil man is suspicious of everyone and tumbles into constant trouble" (Prov. 17:20 LB).

4. When, in seeking to be serious, we lose our sense of humor and our positive approach to life. "Rejoice in the Lord alway: and again I say, Rejoice" (Phil. 4:4).

5. When, in our desire to be conscientious, we overemphasize details. Jesus said, "Woe unto you, scribes and Pharisees, hypocrites! for ye pay tithe of mint and anise and cummin, and have omitted the weightier matters of the law, judgment, mercy, and faith: these ought ye to have done, and not to leave the other undone" (Matt. 23:23). "For Moses said, Honour thy father and mother; and, Whoso curseth father or mother, let him die the death: But ye say, If a man shall say to his father or mother, It is Corban, that is to say, a gift, by whatsoever thou mightest be profited by me; he shall be free. And ye suffer him no more to do ought for his father or his mother; Making the word of God of none effect through your tradition, which ye have delivered: and many such like things do ye" (Mark 7:10–13).

6. Christians living in distress because they fear they cannot please God.

B. Spiritual pride.

C. Exclusivism.

D. Using a person, instead of training him or her.

E. Immersing the disciple in activities. Recently, in visiting a Christian work in another country, I had the privilege of spending the evening with the leader and his seven key people. After inquiring as to what they were doing, it soon became apparent that he had the people so busy meeting with him on a personal basis and in Bible studies, that they had no time for ministries of their own. By the time they had fulfilled their obligations to him, to their jobs, and their families, there was nothing left over. We must leave people with time for their own ministries.

F. Becoming locked into a specific training pattern, thus ignoring the disciple's immediate personal needs, natural abilities, and spiritual gifts. Watch out for this. The following allegory about an animal school illustrates the point: The school curriculum consisted of running, climbing, flying, and swimming. All the animals had to take all of the subjects.

The duck was good in swimming and fair in flying, but he was terrible in running, so he was made to drop his swimming class and stay after school to practice his running. He kept this up until he was only average in swimming. But average was acceptable. The others (including the teacher) were no longer threatened by the duck's swimming ability. So everyone felt more comfortable— except the duck.

The eagle was considered a problem student. For instance, in climbing class he beat all others to the top of the tree, but he used his own method of getting there. He had to be severely disciplined. Finally, because of noncooperation in swimming, he was expelled for insubordination.

The rabbit started at the top of the class in running, but was obviously inadequate in other areas. Because of so much makeup work in swimming, he had a nervous breakdown and had to drop out of school.

Of course, the turtle was a failure in most every course offered. His shell was considered to be the leading cause of his failures. So it was removed. That did help his running a bit, but sadly he became the first casualty when he was stepped on by a horse.

The faculty was quite disappointed. But all in all, it was a good school in humility—there were no real successes.

None seemed to measure up to the others. But they did concentrate on their weak points and some progress was made.

The point is that God didn't design everyone to fit the same mold. Don't zero in on people's weaknesses alone. Find out what their strengths are and develop them. Weaknesses can best be overcome in an atmosphere of success.

There are two basic philosophies of helping people, and they are almost at opposite ends of the pole. One of them says, "You come join me, and I'll help you on my terms. I will train you to be part of my team."

The other is found in Acts 16:9, "And a vision appeared to Paul in the night; There stood a man of Macedonia, and prayed him, saying, Come over into Macedonia, and help us." The man didn't say, "Come over and recruit us. Come over and train us." He simply asked for help. This kind of ministry asks the question, "How can I help you develop your God-given gifts to the ultimate, in order that you may fit in your place in the body of Christ and be most effective?"

G. Pushing *methods* rather than *principles*. Policies are many, principles are few. Policies often change, principles never do. We must be careful that we do not allow our policies to shift over into the area of principles. Our stance should be one of flexibility on policy, but steadfastness on principle.

H. Grasping truth on a more intellectual level rather than applying it to life.

In 1 Thessalonians 1:6–9 Paul sums up a method of evaluating progress in the training process:

> Verse 6—responding to the Word.
> Verse 7—exemplary living.
> Verse 8—ministry skills.
> Verse 9—the totally transformed life. See also Matthew 6:33 and Philippians 1:21.

Now that we've looked at teaching and training we

come to the most crucial part of all, building. This deals with character. This is what we really are, when no one else is around. How can we do it? Let's look at it together.

8

How to Make Disciples

Part V: Building

In the construction of buildings, there are any number of types of structures which can be built: anything from the wild imaginings of a Finnish architect to the more traditional structure of a purely functional building. What is it God wishes to build in disciples? Not some nonfunctional person who can spout strange philosophies of the universe; but someone who can manage getting through daily living with a Christ-centered attitude, someone who can handle the problems of living, who has a sane estimate of himself, and who is able to explain his relationship with God to others. The life of Christ is meant to be expressed in the believer.

Building toward godly character

Paul says:

Let no man despise thy youth; but be thou an example of the believers, in word, in conversation, in charity, in spirit, in faith, in purity. Till I come, give attendance to reading, to exhortation, to doctrine. Neglect not the gift that is in thee, which was given thee by prophecy, with the laying on of the hands of the presbytery. Meditate upon these things; give thyself wholly to them; that thy profiting may appear to all. Take heed unto thyself, and unto the doctrine; continue in them: for in doing this thou shalt both save thyself, and them that hear thee" (1 Tim. 4:12–16).

We will use these verses as a basis to discuss godly Christian character:

125

1. *Character is not a matter of age.* Paul told Timothy not to worry about his youth. Elihu said, "But it is not mere age that makes men wise. Rather, it is the spirit in a man, the breath of the Almighty which makes him intelligent" (Job 32:9 LB). "Thy commandment makes one wiser than my enemies" (Ps. 119:98 RSV).

2. *How one talks reveals inner character.* Timothy, in verse 12, was warned to be an example in word. This includes teaching and verbal communication of every kind. One's words reveal one's heart. Learn to read a person's heart in his/her words.

3. *Character expresses itself in conduct.* The word "conversation" in the King James version means "conduct." Paul says, "For God hath not called us unto uncleanness, but unto holiness" (1 Thess. 4:7). Peter adds, "But as he which hath called you is holy, so be ye holy in all manner of conversation; Because it is written, Be ye holy; for I am holy" (1 Peter 1:15,16).

4. *A godly character has godly attributes.* These attributes are love, faith, and purity (see v. 12).

5. *Godly character needs to be fed.* This is done by reading (v. 13) and by meditation (v. 15), and also through the other methods of taking in the Word (see chapter 7, The Necessity of the Word).

6. *One's ministry is developed along the lines of one's spiritual gifts* (v. 14):

a. Everyone has at least one spiritual gift: "God always has shown us that these messages are true by signs and wonders and various miracles and by giving certain special abilities from the Holy Spirit to those who believe; yes, God has assigned such gifts to each of us" (Heb. 2:4 LB). Paul says, "But the manifestation of the Spirit is given to every man to profit withal" (1 Cor. 12:7).

b. No one has all the gifts. "And God hath set some in the church, first apostles, secondarily prophets, thirdly teachers, after that miracles, then gifts of healings, helps, governments, diversities of tongues. Are all apostles? are all prophets? are all teachers? are all workers of miracles? Have all the gifts of healing? do all speak with tongues? do all interpret?" (1 Cor. 12:28–30). Obviously, the answer is no.

c. Gifts are given for helping the whole body of Christ. F. F. Bruce's paraphrase of 1 Corinthians 12:7 reads, "Now whatever form the manifestation of the Spirit takes, every person who receives it receives it for his own spiritual advantage and that of others."

d. Gifts are not a mark of spirituality. Paul says, "Now you have every grace and blessing; every spiritual gift and power for doing his will are yours during this time of waiting for the return of our Lord Jesus Christ" (1 Cor. 1:7 LB). The church in Corinth obviously had every spiritual gift operating. And yet, in the first three verses of 1 Corinthians 3, Paul gives them the most scathing condemnation he gave any of the churches. He told them that they were babes in Christ and that they acted just like the unconverted. From this we conclude that the operation of the gifts of the Spirit, in the individual life or in a congregation, are not necessarily marks of spirituality. The measure of spirituality is the fruit of the Spirit, as pointed out in Galatians 5:22,23.

e. How to help a disciple discover gifts: 1) What does the person like to do? 2) What does God bless that he/she does? 3) How do others see him/her?

7. *Wholeheartedness is a mark of godly character* (v. 15).

8. *Godly character is recognized by others* (v. 15). In Matthew 5:16 Jesus says, "Let your light so shine before men, that they may see your good works, and glorify your Father which is in heaven."

9. *Godly character must be protected* (v. 16). Jesus says, "Watch and pray, that ye enter not into temptation: the spirit indeed is willing, but the flesh is weak" (Matt. 26:41). Paul says, "Watch ye, stand fast in the faith, quit you like men, be strong" (1 Cor. 16:13).

10. *The root from which godly character springs is the thought life* (v. 16). The mind is the real battleground. In Proverbs 4:23 Solomon says, "Keep thy heart with all diligence; for out of it are the issues of life." The word "heart" here means one's inner thoughts. Paul says, "And be renewed in the spirit of your mind; And that ye put on the new man, which after God is created in righteousness and true holiness" (Eph. 4:23,24). "And be not conformed to this world, but be ye transformed by the renewing of your mind, that ye may prove what is that good, and acceptable, and perfect, will of God" (Rom. 12:2).

11. *Godly character takes daily choices* (v. 16). "And he (Jesus) said to them all, If any man will come after me, let him deny himself, and take up his cross daily, and follow me" (Luke 9:23).

12. *God blesses godly character* (v. 16).

13. *God uses those with godly character to help others* (v. 16).

14. *God's standard operating procedure is to change lives and build character.* Paul says, "I have been sent to bring faith to those God has chosen and to teach them to know God's truth—the kind of truth that *changes lives*— so that they can have eternal life, which God promised them before the world began—and he cannot lie" (Titus 1:1,2 LB). "Wherever that gospel goes it produces Christian character, and *develops it,* as it has done in your own case from the time you first heard and realized the truth of God's grace (Col. 1:6 Phillips).

Building begins with clearing away the obstacles to progress

God says, "See, I have this day set thee over the nations and over the kingdoms, to root out, and to pull down, and to destroy, and to throw down, to build, and to plant" (Jer. 1:10).

1. *Root out bitterness, hostility, and fear.* "Looking

diligently lest any man fail of the grace of God; lest any root of bitterness springing up trouble you, and thereby many be defiled" (Heb. 12:15).

2. *Pull down idols.* "Their heart is divided; now shall they be found faulty: he shall break down their altars, he shall spoil their images" (Hosea 10:2) "Mortify therefore your members which are upon the earth . . . covetousness, which is idolatry" (Col. 3:5).

3. *Destroy bad responses.* "And Mary said, Behold, I am the handmaid of the Lord; let it be to me according to your word." (Luke 1:38 RSV). And from the 20th Century New Testament: "Do not think I am saying this under the pressure of want. For I, however I am placed, have learnt to be independent of circumstances" (Phil. 4:11).

4. *Throw down ungodly imaginations.* In 2 Corinthians 10:3–5 Paul says, "For though we walk in the flesh, we do not war after the flesh: (For the weapons of our warfare are not carnal, but mighty through God to the pulling down of strongholds;) Casting down imaginations, and every high thing that exalteth itself against the knowledge of God, and bringing into captivity every thought to the obedience of Christ." The wise writer of Proverbs wrote, "For as he thinketh in his heart, so is he" (23:7).

Clearing away the obstacles involves correction

Correction is only viable when the relationship with the other person is solid and established. The person must know that you love him/her, and that you are pointing out problems not to be critical, but to be helpful. God says, "And if a good man becomes bad, and you refuse to warn him of the consequences, and the Lord destroys him, his previous good deeds won't help him—he shall die in his sin. But I will hold you responsible for his death, and punish you" (Ezek. 3:20 LB).

1. *What 2 Timothy 4:2 says about correction.* The

verse reads, "Preach the word; be instant in season, out of season; reprove, rebuke, exhort with all longsuffering and doctrine."

a. Reprove. This means to expose something in a person's life, developing the conviction that it is a sin. This is the work of God by the Holy Spirit.

b. Rebuke. What does it mean to rebuke? This means to "bawl one out" for letting the matter reach such a state of deterioration.

c. Exhort. This is always connected with the future, not the past; and it is designed to help correct the problem. Exhortation aims at producing the right effect in changing a life.

d. The Scripture is adequate in doing all of the above things: "All scripture is given by inspiration of God, and is profitable for doctrine, for reproof, for correction, for instruction in righteousness" (2 Tim. 3:16).

2. *Five principles of rebuke.* There must always be a proper balance between rebuking a person and loving him or her.

a. If you do love a person, you will rebuke him/her. But it is a two-way street. The person must be committed to you, and you must commit yourself to him/her. If you rebuke, you must be willing to receive rebuke.

b. Find out why the person is walking in error. Generally, you will find it is one of three reasons: either the person doesn't see the thing, or the person is in rebellion, or he/she is trying to obey but can't. A careful and prayerful determination of which of these is true must be exercised.

c. Rebuke on the basis of impression, not accusation. Never go to a person and say, "You did such and such." It is better to say, "You know, it seems to me that in this situation, this is the way you responded or acted. Is that right?" Give the person the opportunity to explain the situation without being accused. In Matthew 7:1 Jesus says, "Judge not, that ye be not judged." We have to be extremely careful about this. One paraphrase of Matthew 7:1 says, "Do not self-appoint yourself to be God's Gestapo. God does not have a 'police-the-faith' force. Your self-righteous condemnation of others will bring an equal judgment against you."

d. Always rebuke using the Word of God as the standard for correct behavior. It is the basis of our authority.

e. Be sure you have the disciple's best interests at heart. Be sure you don't have any anger, animosity, or bitterness in your heart. "He that rebuketh a man afterwards shall find more favour than he that flattereth with the tongue" (Prov. 28:23).

Planting a new structure is also a part of building

Three helpful questions to ask yourself in this regard are: 1) What does the disciple need? 2) How can he/she get it? 3) How will I know when he/she has it? If it's a *concept* you're trying to teach, the question would be: 1) What do I want the disciple to know? 2) How am I going to help that person to learn it? 3) How will I know when it has been learned? If it's a *training* situation, the questions would be: 1) What skill do I want the disciple to develop? 2) How will I train the person in that skill? 3) How will I know when the skill has been acquired? If it's in the area of *character-building,* the questions would be: 1) What trait of character do I want the learner to develop? 2) How can I help build this trait into the disciple's life? 3) How will I know when this trait of character has become a part of that person's life?

Everyone is different

All people need some basics in their lives such as love and acceptance, but it is important to determine individual needs in the person: who is this one and where is he/she going? This must be determined before we can seriously begin helping the disciple.

Paul says, "Therefore encourage one another and build

one another up, just as you are doing. But we beseech you, brethren, to respect those who labor among you and are over you in the Lord and admonish you, and to esteem them very highly in love because of their work. Be at peace among yourselves. And we exhort you, brethren, admonish the idle, encourage the fainthearted, help the weak, be patient with them all" (1 Thess. 5:11–14 RSV).

This passage speaks of spiritual leaders:

1. Who are spiritual leaders? (vv. 12 and 13)

    a. Those who labor among you.

    b. Those who are over you in the Lord.

    c. Those who admonish you. The Greek word for admonish is *noutheteo.* This means to "confront."

2. How are we to respond to spiritual leaders? (v. 13)

    a. Respect and esteem them highly.

    b. Respect them because of their work.

3. How to treat different people (v. 14)

    a. The idle? Admonish them. Idle means those who are lazy and unruly. The Greek word for this indicates a military formation where one is out of step with the rest of the soldiers. It is rebellion. The prophet Samuel says, "For rebellion is as the sin of witchcraft, and stubbornness is as iniquity and idolatry" (1 Sam. 15:23).

    b. The fainthearted? Encourage them. The King James version uses the word "feebleminded" here. These are the individuals who run out of steam. They are timid. They know how to do it, and they would like to be able to do it, but they just don't have the courage and motivation.

    c. The weak? Help them. I take this to mean the untrained. These are simply the people who don't know how to do it.

    d. Be patient with all people. Our difficulty in understanding those who are weak where we are strong is simply human nature. It seems so very obvious to us. Be patient.

A strong *warning* here: The verse says to admonish the

idle and lazy. You certainly don't want to encourage them, or they will remain lazy. You don't want to help them, or they will sit down and let you do it all. Don't admonish the timid, those who know how to do it, but just don't have the courage, because if you do, you will crush them. And you certainly don't want to help the timid, because they already know how to do it. This will frustrate them and give them a greater guilt complex. Don't admonish the untrained person. Such a person can't help it; such people don't know how to do it. And don't coddle the untrained. If you do, they will persist in their ignorance. What they need is training.

In working with people remember that you may encounter these various types. This is why it is important to carefully determine where disciples are. They may be untrained in some areas; they may be fainthearted in other areas; or they may simply be lazy. Assess and analyze the situation to know how to deal with it.

Building must be specific and of primary importance in the area of decision-making

1. *Making decisions.* "And Elijah came unto all the people, and said, How long halt ye between two opinions? If the Lord be God, follow him: but if Baal, then follow him. And the people answered him not a word" (1 Kings 18:21). God does not vacillate and He does not want His people to vacillate. In Revelation where God is speaking to the churches, five of them were reprimanded because of their indecisiveness.

Energetic people tend to be more decisive than lethargic people. An energetic person completes one job and immediately picks up another. A lethargic person begins one job and then goes into neutral before attacking another. God expects our yes to be yes and our no to be no . . . not a little bit of each. "Then why, you may be asking, did I change my plan? Hadn't I really made up my mind yet? Or am I like a man of the world who says 'yes' when he really means 'no'? Never! As surely as God is true, I am not that sort of person. My 'yes' means 'yes' " (2 Cor. 1:17,18 LB).

a. Life is made up of choices and decisions: salvation, quiet time, scripture memorization, honesty, moral purity, obedience, honoring parents, honoring mate, and so on.

b. Indecisiveness may reveal five things about a person. It may reveal *immaturity*. The writer of Proverbs said, "A mature man knows the wise thing to do, but an immature person can never decide" (17:24 GNB). Second, indecisiveness may reveal a *lack of facts*. This is laziness. "Get the facts at any price, and hold on tightly to all the good sense you can get" (Prov. 23:23 LB). Third, indecisiveness may reveal a *fear of consequences or people*. Paul writes, "For God hath not given us the spirit of fear; but of power, and of love, and of a sound mind" (2 Tim. 1:7). John said, "For they love the praise of men more than the praise of God" (John 12:43). The unfaithful steward said, "And I was afraid and went and hid thy talent in the earth . . ." (Matt. 25:25). Fourth, indecisiveness may reveal a *lack of convictions*. Paul tells us, "Beware, lest any man spoil you through philosophy and vain deceit, after the tradition of men, after the rudiments of the world, and not after Christ" (Col. 2:8). One who doesn't stand for something will fall for about anything. Again in Ephesians 4:14 Paul says, "That we henceforth be no more children, tossed to and fro, and carried about with every wind of doctrine, by the sleight of men, and cunning craftiness, whereby they lie in wait to deceive." Beware of the various sects, new approaches, new philosophies, new movements, or any group that won't give you a concise doctrinal statement of what they believe right at the very outset. And, fifth, indecisiveness may reveal a *lack of faith*. In Romans 14:23 Paul says, "And he that doubteth is damned if he eat, because he eateth not of faith: for whatsoever is not of faith is sin."

c. Here are four helpful thoughts when indecisive: One, God wants me to know His will. Two, do I know it? If so, I should trust Him and act on it. Three, am I trying to find out? If not, I am kidding myself. And, four, have I found it out? If so, I must get busy and trust him.

d. Here are six insights toward decisiveness: One, *get the facts*. "Get the facts at any price, and hold on tightly to all the good sense you can get" (Prov. 23:23 LB).

Two, *face the facts*. "But Naaman was wroth, and went away, and said, Behold, I thought, He will surely come out to me, and stand, and call on the name of the Lord his God, and strike his hand over the place, and recover the leper" (2 Kings 5:11). He "thought." One characteristic of straight thinking is facing the facts once you get the facts. "The wise man looks ahead. The fool attempts to fool himself and won't face facts" (Prov. 14:8 LB). We can avoid the vagueness with which many people live if we become explicit and can tell the difference between what we know and what we don't know. We mustn't sit on the fence, never committing ourselves, never making any decisions. Doing nothing has consequences just as surely as doing something has.

Three, *plan ahead*. "We should make plans—counting on God to direct us" (Prov. 16:9 LB). "For want of skilful strategy an army is lost; victory is the fruit of long planning" (Prov. 11:14 NEB).

Four, *think through*. "A prudent man foresees the difficulties ahead and prepares for them; the simpleton goes blindly on and suffers the consequences" (Prov. 22:3 LB). "The simple believes every word, but the man of insight makes sure where he is going" (Prov. 14:15 MLB). People who seem most balanced and most efficient when times get tough are the people who have figured out the very worst thing that can happen, have faced it and decided what to do if it does happen. Then anything else that happens will be an improvement.

Five, *make a decision*. Paul asks, "For if the trumpet

give an uncertain sound, who shall prepare himself to the battle?" (1 Cor. 14:8).

Six, *do it now.* This applies to all the above points. Get the facts now. Face the facts now. Plan ahead now. Think through now. Make a decision. Do it now. People who hesitate in making a decision are in a most unfortunate position. By remaining in the middle of the road, they face the danger of being run over by both lanes of traffic instead of just one!

2. *A positive outlook.* Paul urges us, "Finally, brethren, whatsoever things are true, whatsoever things are honest, whatsoever things are just, whatsoever things are pure, whatsoever things are lovely, whatsoever things are of good report; if there be any virtue, and if there be any praise, think on these things" (Phil. 4:8).

Victory tends to favor the contestants who fight under the positive banner. They are people who have trained themselves to think "What action am I going to take?" instead of "What is going to happen to me?"

Desiring something is more than just having a willingness to accept it if it comes your way. It is positive and purposeful, energetic and creative action. It is empowered by initiative, energy, and perseverance . . . and all of these are positive forces.

3. *Perseverance.* Most people differ less in capacity than in zeal and determination. They should utilize the powers they have. Great works are often performed not by strength, but by perseverance.

> Two frogs fell into a deep cream bowl.
> One was an optimistic soul,
> But the other took the gloomy view.
> "We shall drown!" he cried, without more adieu.
> So with the last despairing cry,
> He flung up his legs and said, "Good-bye."
> Quoth the other frog with a merry grin,
> "I can't get out, but I won't give in!
> I'll just swim around until my strength is spent,

And then when I die, I'll be more content."
Bravely he swam until it seemed
That the struggle had begun to stir the cream.
On the top of the butter, at last he stopped,
And out of the bowl he gayly hopped.
What is the moral? 'Tis easily found.
If you can't hop out, keep swimming around.

—*Unknown*

4. *Relating to business associates.* Win the right to be heard in the business community. Let others see your good example in the way you conduct your business. They can understand that language.

5. *Relating to the church.* Always serve with respect, realizing that when all our ad hoc Christian movements have come and gone, the local church, in my opinion will still be there to house the body of Christ.

In building, your own life is the greatest tool you can use with your associates. In Philippians 4:9 Paul says, "Those things, which ye have both learned, and received, and heard, and seen in me, do: and the God of peace shall be with you:" He also wrote to Timothy: "But thou hast fully known my doctrine, manner of life, purpose, faith, longsuffering, charity, patience, Persecutions, afflictions, which came unto me at Antioch, at Iconium, at Lystra; what persecutions I endured: but out of them all the Lord delivered me. Yea, and all that will live godly in Christ Jesus shall suffer persecution. But evil men and seducers shall wax worse and worse, deceiving, and being deceived. But continue thou in the things which thou hast learned and hast been assured of, knowing of whom thou hast learned them" (2 Tim. 3:10–14).

Marks of a spiritual person

1. *The desire to be holy, rather than happy.* "For God hath not called us unto uncleanness, but unto holiness" (1 Thess. 4:3).

2. *The desire to see the honor of God advance through*

one's life, even if it means suffering temporary dishonor or loss. Paul says, "Whether therefore ye eat, or drink, or whatsoever ye do, do all to the glory of God" (1 Cor. 10:31).

3. *The desire to carry one's cross.* The cross is that extra adversity that comes to us as a result of our obedience to Christ and identification with Christ. This cross is not forced upon us; we voluntarily take it up with the full knowledge of its consequences. "And he (Jesus) said to them all, If any man will come after me, let him deny himself, and take up his cross daily, and follow me" (Luke 9:23). Jesus said, "These things I have spoken unto you, that in me ye might have peace. In the world ye shall have tribulation: but be of good cheer; I have overcome the world" (John 16:33). Paul says, "Yea, and all that will live godly in Christ Jesus shall suffer persecution" (2 Tim. 3:12).

4. *Such a one sees everything from God's viewpoint.* In Colossians 1:9,10 Paul writes, "We are asking God that you might see things, as it were, from His point of view by being given spiritual insight and understanding. We also pray that your outward lives which men see, may bring credit to your master's name and that you may bring joy to his heart by bearing genuine Christian fruit, and that your knowledge of God may grow yet deeper" (Phillips, italics mine).

5. *Such an individual would rather die right, than live wrong.* Such a person will not purchase a few extra days of life at the cost of compromise or failure. Daniel 3:16–18 is perhaps the greatest biblical example of this: "Shadrach, Meshach, and Abednego, answered and said to the king, O Nebuchadnezzar, we are not careful to answer thee in this matter. If it be so, our God whom we serve is able to deliver us from the burning fiery furnace, and he will deliver us out of thine hand, O king. But if not, be it known unto thee, O king, that we will not serve thy gods, nor worship the golden image which thou hast set up."

6. *A willingness to see others advance at one's own expense.*

7. *Such an individual habitually makes eternity judgments instead of time judgments.* Such a person would rather be useful than famous—would rather serve than be served. "He (Moses) considered the 'reproach of Christ' more precious than all the wealth of Egypt, for he looked steadily at the ultimate, not the immediate, reward" (Heb. 11:26 Phillips). At the end of this chapter is a disciple-rating sheet. Let me suggest that you rate yourself from the various items listed and then honestly rate the person or persons you are working with. You may be surprised to find, in fact, that you have reproduced your own weakness. Jesus said, "Go, make disciples."

Disciplemaking is the greatest challenge for the Christian. Getting intimate personal help is one of the single greatest privileges a young Christian can have. And it is all for the accomplishment of the greatest commission ever given to man: The Great Commission calls us to go into the whole world and make disciples of all people. In this book I have tried to share my life, my successes, my failures, and what little I have learned about being a disciple of Jesus Christ and making disciples on my own pilgrimage of faith. I pray that this volume will help you to be a better disciple of the Master and a better disciplemaker.

Disciple-rating Sheet

On a scale of 1 to 10 (1 being very weak, 10 being very strong) evaluate yourself and then, the person with whom you are working in the areas of Vision, Ministry Skills, and Character.

	weak					avg.				strong	undecided	
Vision	1	2	3	4	5	6	7	8	9	10	X	Comments
1. Grasp of what follow-up is												
2. Grasp of multiplication principle												
3. Understanding what it means to motivate, teach, train, and build												
4. Understanding and obeying the great commandment. Matthew 22:36–40												
5. The Great Commission being his vision												
6. An understanding of world need												
7. Understands every person's need for Christ												
8. An understanding of the world situation—political, economic, religious												
9. A grasp of population centers, degree of evangelical witness, present response												
10. An understanding of what God has done in the past												
11. The infinite worth of the individual												
12. The absolute authority of the Bible												
13. Prophecy—what is going to happen												
14. Reality of heaven and hell												

Ministry Skills

	1	2	3	4	5	6	7	8	9	10	X	Comments
1. Personal testimony												
2. Evangelism												
3. Public speaking												
4. Ability to encourage others												
5. Specific application of the Word												
6. Ability to lead a group Bible study												
7. Scripture memory												
8. Helping another one-to-one												
9. Ability to set objectives												
10. Takes steps to reach objectives												
11. Prayer life												
12. Quiet time												
13. Ability to prepare Bible Study												
14. Ability to work on a team												
15. Initiative to do things independently												
16. Ability to motivate people												
17. A thinker												
18. Balance												
19. Peacemaker												
20. Leader												
21. Creative												
22. Ability to work with those who disagree												
23. Flexible												
24. Organizational ability												
25. Sensitivity to sin												
26. Sensitivity to needs of others												
27. Sensitive to others' response toward him												
28. Pacesetter												
29. Recognizes spiritual gifts												
30. Develops spiritual gifts												

Character	1	2	3	4	5	6	7	8	9	10	X	Comments
1. Honest												
2. Faithful												
3. Servant heart												
4. Mannerly												
5. Relates well to opposite sex												
6. Relates well to own sex												
7. Good attitude toward possessions												
8. Wise use of money (financially responsible)												
9. Generosity												
10. Good relationship with parents												
11. Good relationship with spouse												
12. Open (not playing games and hiding)												
13. Hard worker												
14. Humility												
15. Patience												
16. Teachable												
17. Not easily discouraged												
18. Will sacrifice to be available												
19. Faith (believes God)												
20. Forgiving												
21. Self-confident												
22. Appreciative												
23. Hospitable												
24. Cleanliness												
25. Good personal appearance												
26. Positive attitude												
27. Loving spirit												
28. Enthusiastic												
29. Gentle												
30. Steadfast												
31. Prompt												
32. Joyous												
33. Integrity												
34. Tenacity i.e. a finisher												
35. Reliability												
36. Decisive												
37. Consistent												
38. Stability												
39. Dependability